Andrew Jefford's

WINE COURSE

Andrew Jefford's
WINE COURSE

ANDREW JEFFORD

with photography by
WILLIAM LINGWOOD & ALAN WILLIAMS

RYLAND
PETERS
& SMALL
LONDON NEW YORK

For Paula, John and Joe: fellow travellers on the journey.

Senior editor   Clare Double
Senior designers   Lizzie Ballantyne and Toni Kay
Picture research   Jess Walton
Production manager   Patricia Harrington
Art director   Leslie Harrington
Publishing director   Alison Starling

Styling   Liz Belton and Róisín Nield
Hair and make-up   Marie Coulter

First published in the UK in 2008
by Ryland Peters & Small
20–21 Jockey's Fields
London WC1R 4BW

and in the US by Ryland Peters & Small, Inc.
519 Broadway, 5th Floor
New York, NY 10012
www.rylandpeters.com

10 9 8 7 6 5 4 3 2 1

ISBN: 978 1 84597 723 8

Printed and bound in China.

A CIP record from this book is available from the British Library.

  Library of Congress Cataloging-in-Publication Data
Jefford, Andrew.
  Andrew Jefford's wine course / Andrew Jefford with photography by William
Lingwood & Alan Williams. -- 1st US ed.
    p. cm.
  Includes index.
  ISBN 978-1-84597-723-8
  1. Wine and wine making. 2. Wine tasting. 3. Viticulture. I. Title. II. Title: Wine
course.
  TP548.J439 2008
  641.2'2--dc22
                                                            2008022097

Contents

Wine: So What?

Our love for wine is in part a love for the earth itself. Our enchantment at wine's beauty mirrors what we feel about our own being on the earth.

The darkness is pricked with starlight. The vines wait. An owl glides out from an oak, listening for mice. The moon meanders across the night sky, ramped above a distant line of hills. Rose, eventually, seeps into the horizon. For 16 hours, the sun arcs overhead, swelling, then abating. The quality of that light changes every few minutes; every day, too, the sun looks down on the vines from a different angle. As the red embers subside, darkness floods the vine rows once again. The stars return. The owl wakes.

All of this happens 365 times in succession before the pattern is repeated; and that pattern may repeat itself 150 times before the vine loses its grip on life. Clouds, wind, rain, frost and snow lay hold of the plant, though none is as implacable as the white sun in searing summer. No wonder the vine is gnarled.

Under the soil, the vine is as tall as a tree. For those 150 years, its roots search out food and moisture in a lightless sky of minerals: here damp clay, there dry sand; here fractured granite, there fissured limestone. Wine is the song of the earth. Much of the music is written by those roots slowly pervading the rock, and their leaves unfurling in the light above.

Vines, indeed, can only experience their place on earth. It's prison and playground by turn. Their life's work is survival and reproduction in that place. Their biography is a saga of endured weather. So, too, for the plum tree; so, too, over one season, for the barley blade, the carrot, the bean. There is, though, one important difference between the wine vine and the bean.

Beans taste of beans. The fruit of wine vines tastes … like grapes, initially. Turn those grapes into wine, though, and differences begin to become apparent. You can taste the grape's genotype: Cabernet Sauvignon, say, or Chardonnay. You can taste what has happened to the grapes and their juice as they were transformed into wine. You can taste the weather during their growing season. And, most movingly of all, you can taste the place on earth in which those vines have passed their ever-lengthening lives.

If you have ever wondered just why there are so many different bottles of wine for sale, dwarfing the range of fruits or meats or even cheeses which the earth offers us, that is the reason. Wine is difference.

Wine, indeed, is the product among all of those we eat and drink which comes closest to reflecting humanity itself. No two people are exactly alike. No two wines are exactly alike, either. Much of the joy of being alive comes from meeting, observing and listening to other people; and much of the joy of wine comes from tasting the multitude of differences between them. For winemakers, too, this pleasure of diversity is paramount. 'Trying to describe places by sculpting liquid is a fascinating job,'

says wine-creating consultant Stéphane Derenoncourt. The freshness of the northern European spring is hidden like a coiled spring inside bottles of Mosel Riesling; the stark white light and palm-scattered openness of Andalucia translates into burnished, coppery Oloroso; the sappy exuberance of New Zealand's garden islands uncurls, fernlike, in its Sauvignon Blanc wines; Australia's ancient earth, broken and reddened by millions of years of solar abrasion, liquefies into black, salty Shiraz. Our love for wine is in part a love for the earth itself. Our enchantment at wine's beauty mirrors what we feel about our own being on the earth, here and now, surrounded by phenomena for which the only appropriate response is astonishment.

The drawback to this small universe of differences is that wine is necessarily complicated. Dozens of countries; tens of thousands of producers, all of them producing a new vintage every year: this is something that cannot be simplified. Nor can astronomy; nor can history. Nothing which respects the innate complexity of the universe and of human activity is ever simple. To simplify is to falsify.

There are ways, of course, to keep the complexity of wine at bay. You could settle for buying nothing but familiar names and brands; you could restrict yourself to the wines of a certain region, or a particular producer. Wine does not have to be enjoyed for what it can tell us about a place on earth; it can also be enjoyed because it tastes nice, and its alcohol helps the drinker set aside his or her cares for a while. If that's enough, you don't need this book.

If, though, you want to explore, discover and relish the beautiful diversity of the wine world, this Wine Course is designed to be a starting point. Tackling the 20 Projects that follow won't tell you everything about wine. That implies a lifetime's study. (I'm still learning, too.) This book will, though, map the land, and give you the grounding you need to explore wine with confidence for yourself. It will answer some of the many questions that every wine drinker asks sooner or later. Maybe it will give you a taste for wine knowledge, to match the taste you already have for wine itself. It will, I hope, give you a safe start to a long journey – not just into the sensual pleasures of wine, but also into its geographical finesse and its cultural depth. The Greek narrative poet Homer drank wine by the firelight; so, too, does his hero Odysseus, freighted with crises. When you or I drink wine by the firelight (perhaps burdened by crises of our own), we join them in an unbroken thread, and we feel richer for doing so.

Remember, though, that there is no destination at the end of this long journey. The journey is everything. No state is steady; no world is static. Everything in wine changes every year, thanks to the play of the seasons and the defining frenzy of human activity. In the longest view, climates change; the earth moves. We can take nothing for granted. Wine is a gift to us, in our time. Let us cherish it, celebrate it, understand it – and in so doing, come closer to our earth.

There is no destination at the end of this long journey. The journey is everything.

- PORTA DOS CAV
(1997) PORT

- CHATEAU LA G
(2005) PESSAC-LE

- SAINT TROPE
(2006) VINDE
FR

- CRET T
(1999)

THE TOOLS

Perhaps 'love' is too forceful a word ... but if you're reading this, then it's safe to assume that you like wine. Moving from that simple sensual enjoyment to an understanding of wine is no different from any other task: it requires tools. Some of these tools have a physical form, like good glassware. Most of the tools, though, are mental – like knowing what to look for in wine, for example; or discovering ways to remember the character of wines you have already drunk. There are practical issues, too. Wines, like children, need a careful upbringing if they are going to realize their potential: what's the best way to look after your bottles once you have bought them? And how do you share your pleasure in wine, and expand your newly acquired understanding of it at the same time? Glasses may break, of course, and need replacing. The rest of the toolkit acquired in our first three Projects, though, should last a lifetime.

**PROJECT 1
HOW TO TASTE**

In this Project, we'll track down some good wine glasses first of all. It will then be time to begin opening bottles, and discover what the wine inside is like. Colour, aroma, flavour and texture are the elements that constitute a wine's personality. Once you have learned to analyse those in turn, you'll have passed your first exam. You'll be a wine taster.

Glasses and Decanters

You could drink wine out of ceramic cups, of course, but wine's visual beauty is such that most prefer the limpidity of glass. Once you begin tasting, though, you'll soon discover that not all glasses are born equal.

Squat, tall, chunky, slender, plain, coloured, engraved, antique, modern: there are almost as many glasses as there are drinkers. For dinner, choose any you like. If an antique glass with a tall, ornate brown stem and a tiny, straight-sided green bowl around which engraved mermaids decoratively tussle with dolphins intensifies your drinking pleasure, then use it.

For tasting, by contrast, try something different. Here's the ideal profile.
+ It's made of plain, clear, uncut glass.
+ It's capacious. Big enough, say, to pour a 100 ml sample for tasting, or a 250 ml serve for drinking, and be able to swirl the wine in the glass without any danger of its slopping onto the tablecloth or your clothes.

+ It's tulip-shaped.

And that's almost all there is to it. Amply rounded glasses are perhaps best for old reds and fragrant reds (such as burgundy); taller, narrower tulip shapes are better suited to aromatic, unoaked whites (like most Sauvignon Blanc or Riesling wines). Sparkling wines and Champagne are best served in the very tall, narrow tulip-shaped glasses often called 'flutes'; a tight point at the base of the bowl will make the line of bubbles twist upwards in a pretty spiral. But I'm already in danger of complicating what should be a simple matter.

After glasses, consider decanters. Don't worry: there's nothing arcane or tricky about decanters. They're helpful; they add to the fun of wine drinking; and they're easy to use. They needn't be expensive, either. A simple glass jug makes a cheap and satisfactory decanter. Once again, clear glass is best; the shape doesn't matter much.

Why decant? For three reasons.
+ To remove an old wine or vintage port from its sediment.

ABOVE Even tulips come in many shapes and sizes. I usually pour about as much as you see in the central and right-hand glasses: ideal for swirling and aroma appreciation. If you feel it's mean, the left-hand glass shows a very generous serve. Any fuller than that, and you'll lose the aromas.

- To give a young wine air. That air will freshen it up, and open it up, too. The effect is like adding a year or two of extra age to the wine.
- To conceal the identity of a wine – for guessing games about what it might be. Tasting a wine without knowing what it is is called a 'blind tasting'.

Any wine (even Champagne) can be decanted: experiment, and note the differences. But don't leave wine in a decanter overnight, since it will tire more quickly than it will in a bottle.

How do you decant a bottle of wine? Nothing could be easier. If the wine you are decanting has a sediment, it's best to have stored it standing up for a week or two first to let the sediment settle at the bottom of the bottle. Then open and pour gently – but stop as the end of the bottle approaches. The decanted wine will be clear. Empty the rest (sediment and all) into a separate glass, and you'll find the last clear wine can be sipped or tipped off the top of the sediment a few hours later. If the wine has no sediment, just pour it all into the decanter with some vigour.

OF CORKS AND CAPS

Bottles need sealing. Traditionally, cork is used. Corks are punched from the bark of the cork oak tree (*Quercus suber*); they are, thus, renewable and biodegradable. Cork forests form part of an ancient and beautiful ecosystem, chiefly in southern Iberia. The greatest wines created and drunk by humans throughout the course of history have achieved perfection via the minute exchanges of oxygen that cork permits with air over time. Whether cork adds a desirable flavour of its own to old wine is a matter of debate.

Cork, though, has a major failing. Between 2 and 8% of all corks are contaminated with trichloroanisole, or TCA. This dulls or spoils the wine, making it smell and taste of mouldy cardboard, or worse. It is this unpleasant smell and taste which is referred to when a wine is said to be 'corked'. For this reason, glass, plastic and screwcap closures are replacing natural cork. Proponents of glass closures and screwcaps, in particular, claim that not only do they avoid TCA contamination, but they also permit a cleaner, purer evolution of the wine inside the bottle. Some screwcap closures now mimic cork's minute air permeability.

Do screwcaps or glass closures perform better than cork? For young wines to be drunk quickly, yes. For wines to be aged, we don't know. Until a range of the greatest red wines in the world has been aged for 30 years under both cork and its alternatives and the outcomes compared, we won't know. Results from Australia, where screwcaps have been used for museum stock for several decades, are promising.

Colours

Every wine tells its own story. A wine's colour begins that story by setting the scene.

Northern European summers are fresh, so look for glints of green and silver highlighting a watery gold. This is young **Riesling** from Germany's Saar Valley.

California's generous sunshine seems to linger and loll in a glass of its golden **Chardonnay**.

Fine Hungarian **Tokaji** is autumn in a glass. Search out the orange and russet glints of fallen leaves.

Time and warmth make **Madeira**, which explains its walnut and oak hues. This is the antique furniture of the wine world.

The Pedro Ximenez grapes in this syrupy **sherry** have been sun-dried, hence the saturated depth of its African ebony.

The height of the wind-ruffled Provençal hills tints its pink **rosé wines** with a salmon-silver delicacy.

Lavishly **plum-pink wine** from the unfettered warmth of Australia promises exuberance of scent and flavour.

True **burgundy** is coaxed from a brief and sometimes stormy summer and a thin-skinned grape – hence its light, pomegranate red.

The crushed blackcurrant and elderberry tint of fine young **Bordeaux** suggests a decade or more of endurance.

The glowing heat of summer on the earth's oldest continent is reflected in the purple-red of this dense Australian **Shiraz**.

The **Tannat** grape, from Madiran in the south of France, is, as its name suggests, heavily laden with textural tannin, hence the storm-black, leather-jacket hue.

When red wines age, like this old Portuguese **Dão**, their dark red colours lighten to garnet and then brick red.

Wine Tasting Step by Step

Take it easy. Relax. Get ready for a sensual encounter with a new place on earth.

Pour the wine into the glass first, gently and steadily, until it's between a quarter and a third full. That will leave you plenty of swirling room.

Time to take a good look. Tilting the glass as you do so will reveal a spectrum of colour – from deep heart to light rim.

Swirl the wine gently in the glass to release its volatile components. Note its viscosity and depth of colour on the glass sides.

Sniff gently. Let your mind float, gathering notes, allusions and memories from the scents rising from the wine. Take a note or two before they fade.

Now it's time to sip. Try directing the wine onto different zones of the tongue: the tip, the sides, the back. Any differences?

Swirl the wine in the mouth, aerating it if you wish. Note flavour and further aromas; feel the texture; and check the wine's structure, too (see pages 19–21).

Aromas

When you buy wine, you spend your money on scents as well as flavours. Don't let them slip by unnoticed.

Every wine exists as an aroma as well as a flavour. That aroma changes with time. Sometimes it is subdued; at other times, it is powerful. What distinguishes good wines from ordinary ones, and great wines from the merely good, is often aroma as much as flavour. Some wines smell compellingly beautiful, like flowers, woodland or turned earth itself. (Not, though, quite like perfume: the aromas are rarely that crafted or that invasive.)

Great wine aromas are also astonishingly complex – and allusive. By this, I mean that they can suggest other scents with which we are familiar. The scent of oak casks is an obvious example with an evident cause, but wines can suggest a wide range of fruits, leaves, spices, even meat and stones. Almost anything which has an aromatic existence in the natural world can be evoked by wine.

How do you set about assessing a wine's scent? Smell it initially without agitating the glass; later, swirl the glass gently. Allow your mind and your memory to float, undirected. Trust your initial judgement. Take a break; go back later. Note whatever the wine reminds you of. Don't be shy.

Don't be disheartened, either, if you can't instantly spot the long list of allusions typically un-nosed by wine writers and sommeliers. They don't matter. What matters is that you allow the wine to talk to you aromatically, that you derive some pleasure from the interaction, and that it stays with you (as a memory, a note, an experience, an emotion) for future reference. Your education is underway.

LEFT What did I write about this one? Oh yes – a faint note of cardamom hidden among the green apples ... but can I still find it? No matter if not: the scent is as enticing as ever.

Flavours

The taste of wine is like the sound of music: limitlessly various. Learning to analyse those tastes will help keep confusion at bay.

Most flavour is in fact aroma. Our taste buds detect the fundamental components of flavour, but it is the aromatic components of what we are tasting, rendered volatile by saliva and the warmth of the mouth, which paint the picture in all its glorious subtlety. Those aromas are channelled up the retronasal passage between the throat and the nose, and detected by the olfactory bulb at the back of the nose. That's one reason why it's worth holding wine in the mouth for some time and moving it about the tongue and gums; you give those aromas a chance, like blown feathers, to lift off.

Then comes enjoyment – but don't forget analysis, too. Note how sweet or dry the wine is. Measure the role of acidity in creating the structure of the wine: sometimes recessive (in soft wines), sometimes dominant (in hard ones). What kind of acidity is it: sharp, green and slender, or bright, ripe and full? Does the wine have a sinewy quality (this is often called 'vinosity')?

You can read more about wine's textural dimension on the next page: that's another key element of flavour. How vivid and round are the fruit flavours? Does the wine have a milkiness or creaminess? What shape do the flavours create: something tall and deep, like a canyon, or something broad and wide, like a river estuary? Is the flavour flute-like and pure, or rich and orchestral? Can you taste oak wood, or toasty barrel treatments? Too much – or just right?

Taking a wine to pieces and examining its component parts with a watchmaker's care will help you understand the next wine you taste a little better.

What might this wine be? Those pencil shavings and cedar tell me that there's French oak here, probably getting to work on some Cabernet Sauvignon, while the tobacco suggests Merlot, too, as it settles down to age. The liquorice piles on the class: it has to be Bordeaux, doesn't it?

Yes, I know those dark spices suggest red wine at first, but sniff again: the hazel and almond are typical of fuller whites from warmer climates, and coffee, cloves and cinnamon could come from over-ambitious use of new wooden casks. Could it be Chardonnay from Sicily?

Now here's a puzzle: the red fruits suggest a lively red wine, and apricot and fennel hint at Mediterranean origins. That appley acidity and faint hint of asparagus, though, suggest that the grapes haven't quite reached full maturity. Middling marks only. Cut-price Languedoc – or perhaps Chile?

The toast and cream set me thinking of rich California whites which have been aged with their yeast lees … yet that soft meatiness behind the creamy fruit makes me think again. An older white Bordeaux? Something from the Rhône? How about new-wave Pinot Gris from New Zealand?

Textures

You don't just smell and taste wine. You feel it, too. Like you and me, wine has a body and a presence.

You could spend five minutes describing the aromas of a great wine, and another five anatomizing its flavours – but there's still more to say.

How does a wine feel in your mouth? Is it light or heavy? Does it feel granite-rough or marble-smooth? Is there an electric, darting quality to it? Or is it comfortably torpid?

Describing a wine simply in terms of its aroma and flavour analogies is curiously unsatisfying. Wines are more than a frenzy of allusions. They are solid and unitary, like buildings. They have an internal architecture; they have a fabric.

Naturally, there are causes for what we notice when we feel a wine. A large part of the textural dimension of wine is due to tannin. This is a family of compounds that occurs naturally in tree bark, leaves and berries – as natural protection, among other things, against fire, insect attack and bacteria. When placed in the human mouth, tannins feel grippy. Drinking tea and wine are two of the commonest ways in which we encounter tannins, though they're found in all fruit skins, too.

Tannins interact with proteins: that's what happens when you tan leather, or put milk into strong black tea, or enjoy a dark red wine with a plate of roast beef. You, the drinker, feel those tannins soften and relax.

All wines, even white wines, contain some tannic mass – but red wines contain about six times as much as white (see page 73). Other compounds in wine which affect its texture include smooth glycerol, incisive acidity, dense dry extract (the residue of a wine once all its water has been removed), the milky or creamy suspension of yeast lees in wine as it ages, and the warmth and fullness of alcohol itself.

The interplay of all these elements is what creates a wine's architecture – and one of the roles of the winemaker is to make sure that this architecture is as satisfying and harmonious as possible. Your job is to judge how successful he or she has been.

ABOVE LEFT Tip the wine forward to gauge its viscosity (or 'legs') and to check the full colour spectrum.

ABOVE RIGHT Don't ignore the aftertaste: that should be lovely, too, and the longer it persists, the better.

OPPOSITE Talking over your impressions is helpful; everyone notices something different about a wine.

FACT FILE:
How to Taste

Glasses Go for plain glass, tulip-shaped bowls and an overall size which is large enough to swirl in safety.

Colours Every wine's colour tells a story – about its grape variety, place of origin and winemaking method.

Aromas Take your time, and keep the door of your mind wide open.

Flavours Allow flavours the time and space in your mouth to become volatile – then analyse them to see how they fit together.

Textures Don't forget to feel wine. Like you, it has a body.

2

**PROJECT 2
HOW TO DRINK**

None of us wants to taste wine without drinking it. Indeed only in drinking a wine, usually with food, can you truly judge it. If wine has a purpose, it is to parry food and aid digestion; it thus contributes to human health and happiness. Yet wine itself is both a food and a drug. Healthy wine drinking demands discipline and respect.

Wine itself is both a food and a drug. Healthy wine drinking demands discipline and respect.

Moderation

Learning to taste wine means learning to enjoy it for something other than its effect: the basis of all sensible drinking.

The doctors are in near-agreement: alcohol can be good for you. Only, though, if it is consumed in moderation. Best of all, it would seem, is red wine rich in tannins, consumed slowly, with food.

What, though, does 'moderation' mean? Humans come in all shapes and sizes. Moderation for a scaffolder is not the same as moderation for a ballerina. Learn to listen to your body, especially after you have drunk wine. If your digestion is good, your sleep sound and you wake with no trace of a headache, then your consumption is unlikely to have been excessive. If your well-being feels compromised in any way after wine, though, drink less next time.

Be tough rather than lenient with yourself. Have alcohol-free days from time to time, and compare the way you feel on those days with the way you feel after you have drunk alcohol. Learn to sniff, sip and savour rather than gulp and swig. Making tasting notes can slow your drinking; buying a wine which costs more than you would normally pay will not only expand your horizons, but decrease your intake. There's nothing wrong with leaving a bottle unfinished until the next day; indeed, a nightful of air may improve it. Those strapping, tannin-laden red wines which cardiovascular researchers favour (like France's Madiran, Italy's Barolo or much Argentinian Malbec) are particularly good on the second day of opening, and sometimes even the third.

Always have a glass of water to hand as you taste and as you drink; never feel obliged to drain a preferred glass of wine to the last drop if you don't want to. It's better to throw wine away than to drink too much. Being a good host sometimes means providing wine-loving friends with some special bottles – but it always means respecting their health. Never cajole anyone into drinking more than they want.

Meditation

Wine is more than an alcoholic drink. Tasting wine to the full means tasting its history, its symbolic power and its reconciling force.

The vine, above ground, is a dwarf; its deep roots in the rock make it a giant. So with human culture. Our present lives are just a breath compared to the awesome chorale of history. The past is finished and gone, of course; yet without it, our existence would be senseless.

Wine has played an influential role in much of that history. There are no more important books for Western culture than Homer's *Odyssey* and the Bible; wine trickles through the pages of each, sustaining when consumed in moderation, destroying when consumed to excess. (The Greek playwright Euripides allows Dionysus to describe himself as 'Most terrible, though most gentle, to mankind.') Wine's part in the Christian Eucharist, symbolizing the blood of Christ, could hardly be more central; in

Jewish tradition, too, wine is seen as a blessing and a symbol of happiness, though never uncomplicatedly so.

For the Ancient Egyptians, wine was the drink of elegance and aristocracy – whereas beer built the pyramids. There is a distinguished strand of Bacchic poetry within Persian tradition, most memorably articulated in the sly quatrains of the mathematician and astronomer Omar Khayyám. As metaphors, wine and intoxication are cornerstones of Sufi rapture. For the Chinese poet Li Bai (Li Po or Rihaku), one of 'the eight immortals of the wine cup', wine drinking is in itself a kind of poetry, effacing the ego and clarifying perception, underscoring the beauty of the world yet at the same time facilitating freedom from attachment.

Those who plant vineyards echo Noah; those who enjoy an evening of firelight, wine and storytelling share in what was, for Homer, the best of life. This history lies in every glass. If wine commands a reverence which other drinks rarely attain, these cultural roots are the reason.

Wine trickles through the pages of the *Odyssey* and the Bible, sustaining when consumed in moderation, destroying when consumed to excess.

ABOVE LEFT The vine provides many of the best-loved design motifs of the ancient world: familiar and reassuring.

ABOVE RIGHT Vineyard work is hard but rewarding. At best, it's closer to gardening than agriculture.

OPPOSITE Wine itself can be a clock by which we gauge the passing of the years.

Expense

Wine costs money. Books, paintings and music, which cost money too, can be repeatedly appreciated and enjoyed; to enjoy wine, by contrast, you must destroy it. Buy carefully.

The price of wine is a paradox. Expensive wines are not always better than cheaper wines. When expensive wines are better, they are often better by a smaller margin than their price would suggest. The finest wines of all are bought as a financial investment, since global demand outstrips supply; this has raised their price to levels which many experienced wine drinkers consider unreasonable.

So what can we say with certainty about the pricing of wine? Three things.

♦ Inexpensive wine can be good wine. If good wine is good enough for you, you never need buy an expensive bottle.

♦ Great wine, by contrast, is never cheap. If you want to taste the greatest wines of all, you must try expensive bottles. This, though, is a hazardous business, since expensive wines are unreliable. The best will expand your wine-drinking horizons dramatically; the worst will disappoint.

♦ Attractive value for money tends to be found among mid-priced wines.

Since most of us are interested in value, let's look further at this third category. In a cheap bottle of wine sold, for example, in the United Kingdom, the wine itself accounts for around 10% of the purchase price. The rest is accounted for by the retailer's profits, taxes, packaging and transport. Since at least some of these costs are fixed, buying a mid-priced bottle of wine means that you are paying comparatively more for the wine itself, and less for these ancillary costs.

Smaller producers of wine can never compete with larger producers on price. Generally, though, the highest quality comes from smaller producers rather than larger ones. The mid-priced range is where smaller producers compete most keenly with one another.

Those who are forging a reputation, and trying hardest to make wines of high quality, will allow the market to reward their efforts. Eventually, the market will crown those efforts with high prices. At the beginning of their ascent, though, their quality will be more attractive than the market price suggests. At least some of tomorrow's expensive wines are today's mid-priced wines.

The price of the most expensive wines is driven up by rarity alone. Rarity has no aroma or flavour. Mid-priced wines are not rare – or not yet. What you pay for is aroma and flavour alone.

You should never, of course, spend more than you can afford on a bottle of wine. You should, though, never spend less than you can afford either. Cheap wine often holds those producing it in a poverty trap; your buying better wine allows them to progress, and enriches wine culture more broadly. In purely sensual terms, it usually provides the drinker with more profound satisfaction, too.

Cheap wine often holds those producing it in a poverty trap; your buying better wine allows them to progress, and enriches wine culture more broadly.

OPPOSITE The big stack of bottles shows how fine wine is kept in the producer's cellar: lying down in the cool darkness, sometimes for decades. Vintages are key: only the great years endure, and the very finest wines are sometimes wrapped for sale, like cashmere scarves, in tissue paper. When you see a wooden rather than a cardboard box, expect expense.

FACT FILE: How to Drink

Moderation Drink less, but drink better. Match glasses of wine with glasses of water; sip slowly; leave a little in the bottle for tomorrow.

Meditation Remember that wine is not just an alcoholic drink: it links us to poets, storytellers, and great religious teachers, too.

Expense Match your wine buying to your resources – but bear in mind that value is greatest towards the middle of the price spectrum.

PROJECT 3
HOW TO LEARN

There's no point in taking a course if you don't want to learn. If you had a perfect memory, and limitless financial resources, then a lifetime's drinking would be as good an education as any. Most of us, alas, have neither. This Project will help you make the most of what you've got.

Remembering and Writing

It is worth taking notes on the wines you taste. Well-ordered notes provide a log of your drinking; more importantly, they will structure your learning.

A bottle of wine is an event. When it's over, nothing remains – save your memory of its aromas and flavours. Memory, via note-taking, can be shared. Notes endure.

When we enjoy wine, we take it into ourselves: an act of great intimacy. For a while, we are inhabited by that wine, with its distinctive body and sensory presence. This intercourse can create astonishingly vivid memories. Many who love wine can recall bottles they enjoyed 30 or 40 years earlier. Tasting and drinking those wines was an epiphany. Like great poems or great pieces of music, they left the soul so ruffled that life was never the same again. For a moment, the drinker seemed to taste stony earth, a certain landscape, an entire summer, a state of rapture. Experiences of this sort often lie at the start of a lifelong passion for wine.

Most wine drinking, though, is not like that. If you taste 20 wines over the next month, memory alone may, six months later, salvage three or four; after that, all is lost. That's why it is worth taking notes on the wines you taste. Well-ordered notes (and it is all too easy to be disorderly) provide a log of your drinking; more importantly, they will structure your learning. The act of note-taking will often help you notice things about a wine which would otherwise have passed you by.

Notes are usually divided into appearance, aroma and flavour; don't ignore texture and structure, either. If you have time, jot down other details about the wine, like information about vineyard or winemaking taken from the back label. Don't ape the language of critics if you don't want to; express what you are noticing in your own way, and as vividly as you can. Scores are, philosophically, hard to justify – but they're a useful shorthand to your true enthusiasm for a wine. Whether you score out of 10, 20 or 100 matters little. You will probably be drinking the wine with a meal after having tasted it on its own first, and it's worth writing down any successful (or unsuccessful) food matches for next time.

Reading

Wine is complicated. Books explain the complications. Some do so pleasurably; many, though, are simply there to provide information, and to be consulted on a reference basis. A vast and ever-expanding knowledge bank of tasting notes exists, too – on the internet, accessed by search engines or site subscriptions.

Reading about wine adds greatly to its pleasures. Aroma and flavour constitute the core of wine's appeal, but most of us want to know more – about the men and women who make the wine, about their vineyards, about the weather pattern in a particular year. If we enjoy a particular wine, we want to find others like it. If we are contemplating an expensive purchase, we want to know just how highly rated the possible contenders for our hard-earned money are. We may simply want to celebrate wine at a time of day, or a moment in life, when drinking it is

not possible. This is when reading becomes an essential adjunct to tasting.

Books, magazines and websites are all there to inform, inspire and entertain. Because wine is such a data-rich subject, it seems likely that websites (which are infinitely expandable) will take over the reference function of books and magazines. Portability, durability, literary quality and the pleasure of the printed word, though, continue to favour books and magazines.

What about the role of wine critics? Whether you follow these internationally via books, newsletters and websites, or domestically via the columns of newspapers, the advice is always the same. Use critical opinion as a sounding board for your own, but remember that no critic is 'right'; each is (or should be) simply consistent and truthful to his or her own palate. That is why critics don't necessarily agree with each other. Every palate is unique – yours included. Trust your own judgement, or follow a critic whose tastes are close to your own. For you, the greatest critic in the world is you.

Use critical opinion as a sounding board for your own, but remember that no critic is 'right'; each is simply consistent and truthful to his or her own palate.

ABOVE Aromas, flavours, words, memories: sometimes just one sniff can whisk you back years. Wine can be time-travel, unlocking not just the memory of a bottle, but of things long forgotten.

Hoarding

A wine collection is a liquid library. The Italians have a word for it: an *enoteca*. How big, though, should that library be, and what creature comforts do bottles of wine crave?

Every wine enthusiast wakes up one morning and realizes that he or she now has more bottles in the house than can be drunk at one sitting. At that moment, a wine collection is born.

A few years pass. The same enthusiast now finds bottles crowding out the living space, marching up and down the stairs, and filling every cupboard in the house. This is when you realize that wine is a bulky, heavy and cumbersome possession. It cannot be stored in an album or on a hard drive; it cannot be placed neatly on a bookshelf. Wine, moreover, likes the kind of conditions which humans don't: a steady, cool temperature; darkness; and gentle though well-ventilated humidity. Unless you have these ideal conditions – which in effect means an underground cellar or purpose-built storage facility – any serious wine collection is best stored professionally.

Most of us, though, can enjoy a rotating stock of two or three dozen bottles at home, with every wine resting for two to nine months, even without a cellar. Cupboards and little-used rooms are the best locations: these can be kept dark, free from vibrating machinery, and as cool as possible. Store wine lying down, ideally in a wine rack. Avoid keeping wine anywhere that is warm, or light, or where the temperature varies by more than one degree centigrade per day: the nearer to the centre of the house, and the further from outside walls, the better. Direct sunlight will ruin wine quickly. Storing wine in a kitchen is inadvisable; storing wine in an attic is catastrophic.

WHICH WINES SHOULD I KEEP?

Most wines are meant to be drunk as soon as possible, and almost all wines can be drunk when you purchase them, if you wish. For a few wines, though, it is better to wait. They will not only be more drinkable after some years' storage, but they will also be more beautiful and more articulate. In that sense, you need to wait in order to get your money's worth.

The simplest guide to which wines these might be is price. Any bottle that costs four times more than the cheapest wine on offer is a candidate for extended ageing, especially if that wine is red. (In European wine-producing countries, up the multiple to eight.) In particular, it is almost essential to age great red Bordeaux, and vintage port. Among white wines, fine white burgundy is often disappointing if drunk too soon. Great Riesling, and great Champagne, are beautiful both young and old. Most drinkers prefer white wines made exclusively from the Sauvignon Blanc or Viognier grape varieties, by contrast, when they are young. If in doubt – don't wait. It's better to drink a wine too soon, and enjoy it in full possession of its faculties, than it is to wait too long and find yourself drinking a faded beauty or, worse still, a fleshless skeleton.

ABOVE Spiral cellars can be added to most houses (or garages, or gardens). What do you fancy drinking tonight?

OPPOSITE That Barossa red could wait a year or two, but I wouldn't want the rosé to lose its youthful bloom.

Sharing

The best way to learn is to share your knowledge. No wine friends locally? No problem: compare notes with other wine lovers on the internet.

There is pleasure to be had in drinking wine alone, but it always seems to be multiplied when wine is shared. Wine drinking and conviviality are inseparable. Not only does talking about what you have learned help fix it in your memory, but the knowledge of others can expand your own. There are practical advantages, too. A single wine bottle can provide 20 tasting samples. Buying and tasting communally, therefore, is by far the best way to expand your first-hand experience, and to try wines which you might not feel able to afford on your own.

Dinner parties, wine-tasting clubs and taught courses are all great ways to learn about wine. Those living in remote areas can compare notes with others via the burgeoning number of wine bulletin boards, website forums and blogs. You could taste a wine in the snow-hushed Swedish countryside one evening, post a note on it, and within hours get reactions from drinkers in Texas, Singapore or Melbourne. The wine world has never been less parochial or more international than today; the opportunities for sharing have never been greater.

FACT FILE:
How to Learn

Writing Notes support the fallible human memory. Organize them well to get best use from them.

Reading Essential if you are to understand the hinterland behind the sensations.

Hoarding Most wines don't need it, but the best usually do. Unless you are sure you have ideal conditions, get your wine stored professionally. If in doubt, drink, don't keep.

Sharing This can quickly expand your knowledge and your tasting opportunities.

THE ELEMENTS

The five Projects you will find in this section of the
book cover the fundamental elements common to
all wines: grape varieties; the stones, soils and
changing skies of the natural environment; and what
human beings do in order to grow ripe grapes and
then transform them into a finished bottle of wine.
This, if you like, is the theoretical knowledge all wine
lovers need. After that, we'll be ready to set off on the
final stage of our course: the practical journey into
wine understanding.

**PROJECT 4
GRAPEVINES:
Meet the family**

This book is about one plant species alone: the wine vine, or *Vitis vinifera*. This one species, however, is populated by an extended clan of grape varieties. No aspect of wine knowledge is more useful than understanding the personalities of the main family members – and we'll meet them in a few pages. In this Project, though, we'll discover a little of their family background.

Vines: The Ancient World

The neat rows of vines in a modern vineyard are a sculpture in time: the result of thousands of years of human coaxing and cutting of an unruly plant.

Long before any of our ancestors had fashioned a pruning tool, the vine tumbled and romped through the ancient forests of Europe, Asia and the Americas. Its evolutionary strategy was simple and successful: find a tree to climb, reach the light, set fruit. Birds were the first vine growers. They were grateful, as winter snow began to fleck the grey skies, for the tiny, sour berries, and their wings carried the pips across wide stretches of water, and over mountain ranges. Millions of years of this casual cultivation fell by.

Fast forward to 1003 AD. A seafaring Norse explorer called Leif Ericson left Greenland that year – and sailed west, into uncertainty, with a crew of 35, in search of a fabled land of plenty. Luck was with them; on their third landfall (probably L'Anse aux Meadows in today's Newfoundland), they reached a pleasant area to overwinter. Salmon ran in the rivers; a mild frost lifted, in the quiet of morning, from green grass rather than tundra. Exploration of the forest revealed a profusion of wild grapes, so they called it Vinland: 'vineland'.

This scene, as it happens, had been mythically prefigured thousands of years earlier in Eurasia. No sooner had Noah stepped from his ark 'upon the mountains of Ararat' than he 'planted a vineyard'. The exact means by which lofty, rampant wild vines were disciplined into the fruitfulness enjoyed by Noah ('And he drank of the wine, and was drunken') will never be known, but traces of wine have been found in a Neolithic jar from Hajji Firuz Tepe, a 7,000-year-old archaeological site in Iran's Zagros Mountains, so viticulture was underway by then. Even today, wild vines are prolific in Transcaucasia – that thick throat of mountainous land north of the Zagros, between the Caspian and Black Seas, with Ararat as its Adam's apple. *Vitis vinifera* is almost certain to have originated here, somewhere in present-day Georgia or Armenia. As we'll find out overleaf, though, Noah's vines came to need Leif Ericson's vines later; almost all the wine we drink today can claim parentage from both.

Calling the boundaries in a species as promiscuous and as prone to mutation and hybridization as the vine is not easy. There are at least 10,000 varieties of *Vitis vinifera* itself, and *vinifera* is one of 700 or so vine species in the Vitaceae family. To us, of course, *vinifera* is by far the most important vine species, since it gives us table grapes and dried fruit as well as wine. The most widely planted grape variety in the world, as it happens, is not Chardonnay or Cabernet Sauvignon, but Sultana (Thompson Seedless in the USA).

And we nearly lost them all.

Vines: The Modern World

Have today's winegrowers gone too far in the quest for varietal safety? You, and drinkers like you, will decide – and your decision will create the wine world of the future.

The grape world we know today began with catastrophe. During the 1860s, vines in the southern Rhône Valley began to sicken and die. Within 20 years, most of Europe's vineyards were infected with the insect-induced disease which, by then, had a name (*Phylloxera vitifolii*) but no accepted cure. Production of wine and brandy plummeted.

We now know what happened. The mid-nineteenth century was a time of horticultural enthusiasm; exotic plants skimmed the oceans, including quantities of American native vine species bound for France. These carried with them a tiny, root-feeding insect to which they had long become resistant. Not so Europe's hapless wine vine.

The solution, conceived as early as 1869 and put into wide-scale practice from the late 1880s, was to graft *vinifera* vine wood onto American vine rootstocks. (Creation of hybrid vines also overcame the problem, but the wine made from hybrids often didn't taste good.) Leif Ericson's vines, thus, saved old Noah's from extinction, and nowadays most vine plants are European above the soil and American below it. Just a few parts of the winegrowing world, like Chile and certain regions of Australia, are phylloxera-free, but even here grafted plants are increasingly used as a precaution. There are a few exceptional soils in which phylloxera cannot make headway, like the sands of Colares in Portugal or the volcanic pumice and ash of the Greek island of Santorini.

One century after the phylloxera crisis, a new revolution is underway. In the past, wines were distinguished from one another principally by origin: burgundy, claret or hock dominated wine lists throughout most of the twentieth century. Variety increasingly plays that role. We tend to ask our wine waiters today for a Riesling, a Cabernet or a Merlot. Much of the impetus for this has come from the wine-producing nations of the southern hemisphere, and the trend is a popular one with wine drinkers, since it is simpler to understand varieties rather than origins.

Does this mean that wine drinking in the future will become more monotonous than in the past? Will Chardonnay and Cabernet eventually become the Coca-Cola and Pepsi-Cola of the wine world? I don't think so. Here's why not.

+ The search is always on for new, unusual grape varieties to supplement those widely planted. Some drinkers hunt these down.
+ No wine ever tastes exactly like another, even if it is made from the same grape variety. Winemaking techniques change its profile; so, too, does the location in which that variety grows. We will discover more about this in Projects 7 and 8.
+ Blends of different grape varieties are used to create wines of intrigue and complexity. This has always been practised in some regions of Europe; it is increasingly followed outside Europe, too.

> Will Chardonnay and Cabernet eventually become the Coca-Cola and Pepsi-Cola of the wine world? I don't think so.

PREVIOUS PAGE Thirty years of hard discipline leave most vines feeling gnarled – but it doesn't stop the sap rising every spring.

OPPOSITE The phylloxera louse lives on in these rolling Sonoma hills. Grafted rootstocks defeat its tiny jaws.

FACT FILE: Grapevines

The vine family 700 species, and almost all our wine and vine fruits come from one: *Vitis vinifera*, which alone includes 10,000 varieties.

Birthplace Transcaucasia (Armenia and Georgia).

Achilles heel Susceptible to the phylloxera mite, therefore needs to be grafted onto American-vine rootstocks.

Most planted vine Sultana (Thompson Seedless).

**PROJECT 5
GRAPEVINES:
The magnificent
seven**

We're about to meet the seven grape-variety stars of the wine world.
Three are white; four red. They're not the most planted; brandy
production means that other white varieties play a statistically
important role too. If you want to commit the names and profiles
of just seven to memory, though, choose these.

Chardonnay

Ubiquitous, amenable and adaptable, as hard to dislike as the smile of a child, Chardonnay is for many wine drinkers synonymous with white wine.

If the grape world has a success story, this is it. Most supermarkets stock a dozen cheap Chardonnays. Chardonnay is the lynchpin white varietal for international wine brands. One of the world's best-loved crisp French white wines, Chablis, is made from Chardonnay; so is the gold standard for full-bodied whites: Montrachet. It's a grape name familiar even to non-drinkers. Indeed it's sometimes used as a girl's name – and I've seen shirts branded Chardonnay, too. It is, if you like, a celebrity grape: feted by some, derided by others, recognized by all.

Let's, though, begin with the facts. DNA analysis has proved, oddly enough, that Chardonnay has exactly the same parents as the much sharper Aligoté, the Beaujolais-producing Gamay and the Muscadet-producing Melon. The parents of these four dissimilar siblings are Pinot (a chameleon variety with at least four well-known forms of its own) and the obscure matriarch Gouais Blanc.

Burgundy is home – and the global popularity of wines from here has been the springboard for the grape's celebrity. Any variety that can produce both the stony, mouthwatering Chablis as well as the banquet-like Montrachet, as rich and complex as an Isfahan carpet, has to be worth planting elsewhere. When grape varieties emigrate, though, they sometimes fail to sing. Chardonnay has sung like a nightingale on five continents. It has often rewarded the welcome it found in foreign soils with the greatest white wines they have produced.

It's an oak-friendly variety: oak chips for cheap wine, or barrel-fermentation in French casks for the best. Those vanillins of oak, as well as the milky or creamy flavour left by yeast lees, are as familiar a part of its personality as its fruit flavours, which can vary from lemon and lime in cooler climates to tangerine, apricot and melon in warmer locations. The end result? Buxom, golden whites, so laden with buttery, oaken richness that they need to be spooned into the mouth rather than sipped: that's one extreme. The other is pale, almost enigmatic whites whose complexities need to be teased and prodded out by air or time. The fact that, very often, these differences are due as much to winemaking techniques as to vineyard origin is another reason for Chardonnay's popularity: it leaves plenty of room for human creativity.

Chardonnay, finally, is one of the three key varieties used in Champagne, adding scent and sensuality to blends, as well as making snow-queen Champagnes of unrivalled finesse and charm on its own. Once again, this has fuelled its travels. Wherever ambitious sparkling wine is made, Chardonnay won't be far away.

OPPOSITE Chablis is where Chardonnay reaches a peak of nervy, stony intensity.

FACT FILE: Chardonnay

The look Pale straw yellow to old gold.

The scent Citrus, melon and pale stone fruits; cream or butter; vanilla.

The flavour Hugely variable, depending on ambition and location. Sometimes vivacious, incisive and mineral; often soft, creamy and full; sometimes unctuous and rich.

The texture Occasionally taut and tight, but usually supple and lush.

Key locations Burgundy, Champagne, Languedoc; California, Oregon, Washington; Australia; New Zealand; South Africa; Chile, especially Casablanca; Canada.

The inside track Blanc de Blancs Champagne is made from Chardonnay alone; it's increasingly used in Spain's Cava, too. Look out for cooler-climate Chardonnays from areas such as California's Russian River Valley, Australia's Adelaide Hills and Tasmania, and even Austria, Canada and New York's Long Island: they are changing the way we think about this variety.

Sauvignon Blanc

No grape variety is simpler to recognize than this one, which may be why it divides drinkers. Some love it; others avoid it.

'White' grape varieties, as everyone who has ever bought a bunch of grapes knows, are green. Portugal has a tradition of making 'green wine' (vinho verde), and there are a number of different grape varieties whose name alludes to greenness (like the Portuguese Verdelho, the Spanish Verdejo and the Italian Verdello). None, though, can evoke the worlds of leaf, grass and glade like this one.

The seventeenth-century English poet Andrew Marvell wrote a poem of 'delicious solitude' called *The Garden*. 'The luscious clusters of the vine,' we learn with no little incredulity in verse five, 'Upon my mouth do crush their wine'. Later, after 'stumbling' on melons and falling on grass, the poet finds his mind 'Annihilating all that's made/To a green thought in a green shade'. That vine just has to be Sauvignon Blanc.

Possibly it was. Sauvignon Blanc is a Bordeaux variety (it is, with Cabernet Franc, one of the two parents of Cabernet Sauvignon), and Bordeaux had, since the marriage of Henry II to Eleanor of Aquitaine in May 1152, kept the English middle classes reconciled to the miseries of a world before dentistry and central heating.

Methoxypyrazines would be the modern oenologist's description for Marvell's 'lovely green': the nettle-fresh scent and flavour that seem to shiver inside a bottle of Sauvignon Blanc. Botanists might imagine chlorophyll. Two places conjure this mouthwatering freshness: France's upper Loire Valley (where the regional wine names include Sancerre, Pouilly-Fumé, Menetou-Salon and Quincy) and New Zealand's Marlborough. For all-out leafiness, New Zealand wins. For a stonier, more mineral pungency, the Loire is still ahead, though Marlborough's avant-garde are racing to catch up.

In these two regions, new oak is usually regarded as unnecessary clothing on a wine that is more attractive naked. Elsewhere, however, Sauvignon is given some new-oak treatment, especially when it is blended with other white varieties – like Sémillon, back home in Bordeaux. The result is then a calmer, milkier and mistier greenness.

Sauvignon is now planted in almost as many locations around the world as Chardonnay. Regrettably: no variety is more misplanted than this one. All its thrilling vivacity, in particular, disappears when it is planted in too warm a location. Winemakers are either forced to resort to stratagems such as early harvesting, acidification, the use of enzymes and selected yeasts and (yes, it has happened) the addition of illegal essences in order to approximate the character of cooler-climate Sauvignon – or simply produce a mushy, aimless white wine tasting of tinned peas or boiled sweets.

OPPOSITE New Zealand and France's Loire Valley: a Sauvignon benchmark from each hemisphere.

Riesling

Is sensual appeal everything? Not quite. Wine needs to feed the mind, too. No variety does this more stimulatingly than Riesling.

Riesling is a northerner. This white grape first came to prominence in Germany in the late Middle Ages. From the mid-fifteenth century, Rhenish princelings and bishops began urging Riesling on those tending their lands. They'd tasted its wine as they tore the flesh from roasted partridge legs – and then snapped jewelled fingers for another goblet. Since this is a late-ripening grape variety, though, it was risky to grow. Its wine might enchant in a good vintage, but when the autumn rains came early, Riesling would be still be sitting out on the muddy slopes, feeding the partridges, while other varieties like Elbling and Silvaner were safely bubbling in the vats. Its rise to prominence was slow.

That was then; now the world is warmer. Now Riesling has travelled, to lands where the sun shines with a generosity rarely found at home. Provided that Riesling can take its time in getting to full ripeness (if the days are hot and sunny, it relishes cool nights), then it always produces white wine of intrigue, of singularity, of balance, of challenge. Something else, too. It appears capable of reflecting its vineyard soils with a fidelity beyond other grape varieties. No other wine seems to taste of minerals to the same extent as great Riesling. I say 'seems' – for you can't reveal slate or granite or limestone in wine by analysis. It's not there. What is?

Riesling does tend to have high levels of extract – the non-volatile solids in a wine. It has, as grape juice, lots of sugar and lots of acidity, too. Like Muscat (see page 50) it is high in perfumed, flavoury monoterpenes. It's voluble. It may be the combination of these factors which gives us the impression that, beneath Riesling's enticing fruit spectrum, there is in fact a light wash of dissolved slate or powdered granite.

At home in Germany, it can produce wines in which alcohol is so low it is barely palpable. In its place you seem to taste fresh fruits more perfectly expressed than in nature itself, thanks to the unrivalled tension between sugar and acidity in the wine. Add those mineral after-flavours, and weave in the perfumes of flower, copse and orchard, and what you are drinking barely seems like wine at all, and more like a subtle summary of the natural world. In Australia, Riesling is much stronger, drier and more masterful – but fruits (now tropical – guava, papaya and mango are typical) still dominate its core, while soil and stone cloak its finish. Other locations bring other variations. The main check on Riesling's expansion, in fact, is not a lack of aptitude for new growing locations, but its perplexingly modest crowd-appeal.

One flavour you'll almost never find, though, is oak. New oak and Riesling don't get on. Riesling is an optical lens, pointing at nature. Oak fogs that lens.

OPPOSITE The thinking drinker's choice: Riesling seems to refresh the mind as well as the body.

FACT FILE: Riesling

The look Water-white via silver-green to oily yellow.

The scent Flowers, fruits and stones. The fruits vary from apple, peach, grape, grapefruit and tangerine in cooler climates to mango, pineapple and papaya in warmer zones. Also look for scents of pith, peel and zest.

The flavour The flavours mirror the scents, though mineral tones become more important. Often held in almost electric balance by fresh acidity.

The texture Extreme delicacy and dewy softness in low-alcohol, low-sugar versions to oily richness in those with higher alcohol or sugar levels.

Key locations Germany; Alsace; Austria; Clare and Eden Valleys; USA, especially Washington and New York; Canada.

The inside track Late harvest and Icewine (together with their French- and German-language equivalents) are never better than when made from Riesling: sweet wines, often of tiny yield and great cost, which seem to explode in the mouth, thanks to that diagnostic tension between sugar and acidity.

Cabernet Sauvignon

If the wine world has a commander-in-chief, it's Cabernet: authoritative, recognizable, consistent and enduring.

FACT FILE:
Cabernet Sauvignon

The look Purple-black when young, garnet when mature.

The scent Blackcurrant, plus pencil and cedar when aged in French oak. Blueberry and blackberry in hot conditions; pepper, grass and green pepper when (too) cool. Stones, meat and spice common. Increasingly harmonious with age.

The flavour Concentrated and pure, built on a core of blackcurrant. Amply tannic, yet with a vivid acid balance too. With age, it softens.

The texture Firm and chewy when young; when mature, round and mellow.

Key locations Bordeaux, especially St Estèphe, Pauillac, St Julien, Margaux, Pessac-Léognan; Spain; Italy, especially Bolgheri; Bulgaria; Australia, especially Coonawarra, Wrattonbully, Margaret River; California, especially Napa; Washington; Chile.

The inside track Meritage is a name used for some Bordeaux blends in the USA. Cabernet is widely used in non-Bordeaux appellations in south-west France, including Bergerac. Up to 20% Cabernet Sauvignon is permitted in Chianti Classico.

Cabernet Sauvignon was born in Bordeaux (its father is Cabernet Franc and its mother Sauvignon Blanc). It likes warmth – in order to get its thick blue skin ripe, its juice sweet, and its profusion of pips into reproductive maturity. That means that it won't ripen everywhere in Bordeaux. Where it does ripen there, it is always blended with one or more other varieties. But give it a good summer, basking like a seal out on the great shingle banks of the Médoc, and it rewards its drinkers with red wines in which enduring sturdiness, complexity, balance and beauty combine in what most consider to be the archetype of all red wine. None ages better or more regularly. None combines refreshment, nourishment, stimulation and digestibility quite so memorably. It's every other drinker's favourite wine.

Small wonder, then, that Cabernet Sauvignon has rolled its forces out globally, and with remarkable success. Those thick skins, and the acidity which lingers in its juice over a long summer, mean that good Cabernet Sauvignon is always a dark, forceful, tannic and firmly structured wine. Unlike Riesling, it loves oak – especially the dark warmth of French oak. Its distinctive flavours of blackcurrant, lead pencil and cedar swell and taper as it travels, but are usually recognizable. There's only one thing Cabernet Sauvignon hates: a cool summer.

The greenness intrinsic to the personality of its mother and often characteristic of that of its father then haunts the son. The result is unhappy. Cabernet Sauvignon in which you smell grass, leaf or green pepper, in which acidity has the upper hand over tannin, and in which blackcurrant is paling to redcurrant, means a disappointing summer – or that the grape is planted in the wrong place.

Happily, there are many right places, and each tends to leave its stamp. In the extravagant light and dry warmth of California, Cabernet Sauvignon swells into one of the biggest-boned and most mouthfilling wines in the world. In Chile, by contrast, it is rounder and sweeter than anywhere else, though at its best Bulgaria provides a European echo. Australia's Coonawarra (which is nearly too cool) brings unrivalled purity of blackcurrant perfume. South Africa's best is savoury. Some of the greatest red wines of both Spain and Italy are built partly or wholly from Cabernet Sauvignon; Greece, Israel and the Lebanon can all make plausible headway with it.

Cabernet often likes to captain a team. 'Bordeaux blends' (involving Merlot, Malbec, Cabernet Franc and Petit Verdot as well as Cabernet Sauvignon) tend to be ampler and more complex than Cabernet alone. Australia gets it to work memorably with Shiraz. Only in California does it truly convince on its own, statuesque and complete.

OPPOSITE Youth and age: great Cabernet Sauvignon takes a long-haul flight to maturity.

Merlot

Supple, round-contoured, fleshy and enticing, great Merlot is the most carnal of the world's red wines.

If you like red Bordeaux, then you probably love Merlot. It's the most planted grape variety there; few Bordeaux reds omit it entirely. And in St Emilion and Pomerol – the 'right bank' – it is the dominant grape, to the point that many wines from these regions could in theory be labelled with the variety name alone (for which a minimum of 85% is required in Europe). Great Pomerol and St Emilion are rich, softly textured (even when tannic), dark and pure. In place of Cabernet's blackcurrants, you are more likely to find plums, blackberries and black cherries. When young and fresh, they can seem almost creamy; with time, they grow more meaty and savoury, even truffley. Oak brings notes of coffee and chocolate. It's comely, open and inviting. Sounds hard to resist? That's what millionaires find. Château Pétrus, for many the world's greatest red wine, is a Merlot (it sometimes includes just a kiss of Cabernet Franc). And most new cars cost less than a case of the 1990 Pétrus. It's worth five of mine.

Merlot only has one drawback. It's a lazy traveller. I don't mean it dislikes travelling; in fact, it grows well in new locations. Its early-ripening nature makes it a popular and safe choice for growers, and its generous yield is accountant-friendly. The name is familiar and easy for most to pronounce. So what's the problem? Leave the limestones, gravels and gentle seaside air of Bordeaux's right bank; leave the pointing finger of Pomerol's church spire; leave the dark caves, catacombs and cloisters of St Emilion; and Merlot can't quite be bothered to produce something as oozingly seductive, as viscerally pleasing, or as meatily ripe as back home. Once on the road, its half-brother (Cabernet Sauvignon) seems to try harder. Merlot often settles for being an easy-going, all-purpose red of little decided character. It enjoys the view; it takes life easy. Indeed, the fact that it ripens early and yields well means that, like Sauvignon Blanc, it is too widely planted; over-cropped Merlot from a cool location (there are many in northern Italy and Eastern Europe) is charmless, leafy and anodyne.

To get the best out of Merlot, it needs discipline: low yields, harvesting at full ripeness and crop sorting (it's prone to rot). It will then reward that strictness with wines which don't necessarily have great force of personality, but always seem to blend well, adding a sweetness of fruit and flesh to spikier, more assertive varieties, especially Cabernet and Malbec. Occasionally, too, it will make varietal wines which at least approximate to the plump, full-lipped, soft-fruited Pomerol profile, even if they rarely ignite the fires of lust that Pétrus, Le Pin and La Conseillante are capable of provoking.

OPPOSITE Great Merlot should always have a smooth, lithe quality. Napa versions have more innate power than those from Bordeaux or Chile.

FACT FILE: Merlot

The look Blue-black or red-black when young; deep brick red when mature.

The scent Plum, blackberry and black cherry, sometimes with a creamy overlay; coffee or chocolate when oaked; later meat, spice, truffle, chocolate, Havana cigar. Less good examples are leafy and anodyne.

The flavour Dark fruits and creamy-sweet richness dominate the early years, but a meatiness and rounded, warm stoniness become increasingly apparent. Acids are usually more restrained and tannins softer than for Cabernet, yet fine Merlot has a magnificent inner glow.

The texture Lush, thick-textured yet soft, maturing to smooth and supple.

Key locations Bordeaux, especially Pomerol, St Emilion, Fronsac, Côtes de Castillon; Italy, especially Bolgheri; Switzerland, especially Ticino; Bulgaria; Romania; Moldova; California; Washington; New York, especially Long Island; Chile; South Africa.

The inside track Merlot, like Cabernet Sauvignon, is used in non-Bordeaux appellations in South-West France such as Bergerac.

Syrah/Shiraz

One grape; two names. This is the wine world's greatest actor, capable of extraordinary transformations.

Syrah is what the French call it; Australians know it as Shiraz. Shiraz is also an ancient city in Iran, once wine-loving. Is the grape Persian? Not according to its DNA. Its genes point to two humble French parents: red Dureza from France's Ardèche, and the Mondeuse Blanche from Savoy.

Geographically, the Rhône is home – but even here, Syrah is capable of majestic stylistic breadth. In the windswept, granite-soiled northern Rhône, it creates lean, sleek, dark, perfumed and poised red wines, taut with coiled-spring acidity, ready to gallop down time's corridors. In the hot boulderfields of Châteauneuf du Pape and other southern Rhône sites, by contrast, it metamorphoses into something more languid, fatter fruited and sweeter scented, gentle as a butterfly brushing flower petals.

In the Languedoc, too, it is busy creating new characters. Few grape varieties are better at lifting scent from the earth into the glass than Syrah, and whenever you smile at the recollection of Languedoc's herb-carpeted hillside scrub in a glass of red wine, it's probably Syrah that's fetched the thyme and the rosemary.

What happened to it on its journey to Australia in 1832? Genetically, it would seem, nothing at all – yet the Shiraz planted in the sandy loams of the Barossa Valley and McLaren Vale performs like yet another

grape variety. Its wines can taste richer and denser than almost any rival on any continent: jam-sweet, oil-thick, as intense as a tropical storm. The use of American oak accounts for something of this character, but grape flesh and skins rather more. Within Australia, too, Shiraz keeps assuming new roles: echoing its northern Rhône origins in the Canberra District of New South Wales, for example, or striking a new, strange, intensely Australian pose, rugged with outlaw beauty, in Victoria's Heathcote.

Maybe it's this sympathy for location, and its ability to reshape its personality time and time again, which has made Syrah/Shiraz such a popular choice across the southern hemisphere and in the USA in recent years. Maybe, though, it's also the fact that Syrah doesn't mind sharing the limelight. Blends made by adding a little fragrant white Viognier to Syrah/Shiraz have now become hugely fashionable, based on the seductive Côte Rôtie role model; but few wine lovers would dispute that what Australians call GSM (Grenache, Shiraz, Mourvèdre) can be every bit as satisfying a blend as Cabernet Sauvignon and Merlot. Australia's hallmark Shiraz-Cabernet blends make yet another plausible double bill. Look out for it, too, on the decomposed granites of Chile and South Africa, where it is busy creating new characters, personalities and identities for the future pleasure of the drinking public.

OPPOSITE From gastronomic dinner idol to fun fizz, Syrah/Shiraz is capable of just about anything.

Pinot Noir

Are you ready for the quest for Pinot Noir? It's a long and difficult path, full of difficulties and disappointments. Not everyone stays the course.

Pinot Noir is the poet among grape varieties. Long flowing locks; flashing eyes; exasperating and sometimes childish behaviour redeemed by occasional brilliance. No grape has broken more winemaking hearts than this one.

It's old – probably 2,000 or more years old, originally selected from wild vines. Genetically, it is mutable. At least three of its mutations are important varieties in their own right (Pinot Blanc, Pinot Gris and Pinot Meunier), and its relationship with Gouais Blanc has produced at least four famous offspring (Chardonnay, Aligoté, Melon and Gamay).

It's almost as if all this fecundity has left Pinot with a permanent identity crisis. Planting it for the sake of ambition alone, without any reference to vineyard aptitude, usually results in jangling, garish wine. Pinot Noir fails, on its travels, far more often than it succeeds. Root it in the right place, by contrast, and you might, just might, create a pale, light-bodied red wine which will soar from the glass, seducing drinkers with its floral perfumes and flavours of fruits, of forest underbrush, of warm stones on summer evenings. Its light, graceful tannins brocade rather than weigh down the wine; its fruit flavours are acid-quickened. Yet it lingers in the mouth, seeming to swell with mysterious sweetness towards a finishing crescendo that is much greater than the sum of its parts. Even after you've swallowed, the perfumes continue to lift like an echo.

So where is the right place? A cooler location than the red-winemaking norm: Pinot Noir needs to be teased into performance. Like all poets, it has a thin skin, so careful work in the vineyard is essential, especially in periods of poor weather. It's mildew- and virus-prone. Only in cooler regions can this early-ripening grape loiter towards autumn, amassing complexity of aroma and flavour. It passes swiftly from the hard, tight-lipped inarticulacy of unripeness to a sweet and stewy caricature if overripe. It needs to be coaxed through fermentation with a surgeon's delicacy; errors (too much oak, too much maceration) are invariably punished. Cool locations, too, mean that vintage variations are likely, and vintage variations themselves constantly throw the grape off balance, as everyone who tastes each new vintage from Burgundy will know.

For all these reasons, bottles of red wine made from Pinot Noir tend to be expensive. Is it worth the risk? Yes, because few wines match a wider range of foods (fish included). Yes, because a light-bodied red is always a welcome change in an ever-more full-bodied wine world. And yes, because it might be the one bottle in a thousand which will make you a Pinot slave for life.

OPPOSITE Burgundy and Champagne are close cousins: Pinot Noir is a key grape in both.

FACT FILE: Pinot Noir

The look Pale red to full scarlet; seldom black-red or opaque.

The scent Fresh raspberry, cherry and plum fruits, with a graceful, aerial style; occasionally floral. Often ruffled with oak when young, bringing sweetness and spice. When mature, capable of great complexity.

The flavour Light and intense, with more prominent acidity than tannin. Rich red fruits dominate. With time developing a wide range of allusions – and a surprising inner power.

The texture Smooth and supple yet lively and incisive.

Key locations Burgundy; Oregon; California's coastal regions; Tasmania; New Zealand, especially Martinborough, Marlborough and Central Otago.

The inside track Look out for rich Pinot fruit flavours in Champagne called Blanc de Noirs, and in the house styles of Krug, Bollinger and Veuve Clicquot. Both Pinot Noir and its mutation Pinot Meunier are widely grown in Champagne – but vinified without their skins, giving a white rather than a red wine.

**PROJECT 6
GRAPEVINES:
Biodiversity**

We've met the stars; now meet the rest of the cast. There is no better way to structure your exploration of wine than by tasting and noting sound examples of wines made from the 16 grape varieties I'll describe in this Project. We conclude with a glimpse of 31 more. Our 47 varieties account for almost all wine made in the southern hemisphere, and most of the wine internationally traded in the north. You know a lot already.

Apple-fresh. And, at best, stone-pure, too, for Loire Valley longevity.

Chenin Blanc

Chenin Blanc is, today, more widely planted in South Africa than in its native France; California has extensive plantings, too. It's useful in both places (it retains its acidity in hot weather) but to understand its character start with France's cool-climate originals: look for names like Vouvray, Anjou, Saumur and Savennières. You'll find them in dry, medium-dry, sweet and even sparkling form. Acidity is always prominent, but it is balanced by a honeyed, waxy fullness; fruit notes suggest apple, grapes and early-season orchard fruits. Moist, mossy stones and cool, deep wells provide the mineral context. The best have an arresting intensity, and medium-sweet or sweet versions can, like Riesling, age four decades without tiring. Pay more for a good Vouvray or Anjou; cheap versions taste confected, and lack the grandeur of which this grape is capable.

Muscat

Its perfumes, evocative of oranges, tangerines, crushed spice and lemon oil as well as of grapes themselves, are the base of its attraction.

Like Pinot Noir, Muscat is prone to mutation, and there are at least two major winemaking Muscat varieties: Muscat à Petits Grains and Muscat of Alexandria. (Muscat Ottonel is a crossing with Chasselas, the dark Muscat Hamburg a crossing with Trollinger.) Its musky, come-hither perfumes, evocative of oranges, tangerines, crushed spice and lemon oil as well as of grapes themselves, are the base of its attraction; in flavour terms, by contrast, it is relatively plain and low in acidity. It is sometimes made into a dry white wine (notably in Alsace), but to capture all those perfumes in their freshest, most pristine guise, it's generally best to make it into a sweet, fortified or light, sweet sparkling wine. Most wine-producing countries have fun with Muscat: Greece's Samos, France's Beaumes de Venise, Spain's Moscatels and Australia's Liqueur Muscats are four luscious examples. If you fancy less alcohol rather than more, and a mouthful of nose-tickling bubbles, look out for Italy's Moscato wines; the most famous is Asti Spumante.

Peaches and freesias: an intoxication of scent, even before you've sipped.

Viognier

Back on page 45, I called Merlot 'carnal'. Is there a white equivalent? There is: Viognier. Genetically, the two varieties have nothing to do with one another (Viognier seems to have Italian antecedents); in sensual terms, though, the draw is similar. Of all dry white wines, this can be the lushest, the most glycerous, the most succulent. Viognier is famous for its floral scents (honeysuckle or gardenia), though ginger, peach, apricot and cream can all play a role. Once in the mouth, that scentedness lingers and deepens, meshing with the wine's provocatively textured, silk-stocking extravagance. Acidity is unimportant; a sense of balance, though, can come from the way in which the wine suggests a slow mineral fire at its core. Fifty years ago, the variety was almost extinct; the growers of Condrieu, where it was fighting for stony terrace space with apricot and peach trees, made a last stand. Now it's much planted – in part, to make those highly fashionable blends with Syrah mentioned on page 46, but in part in the hope (sometimes realized, especially in California) that it will unveil its odalisque-like charms. It blends well with other white varieties, too. Don't keep it, though, unless you have a taste for adventure; beauty this precocious doesn't always last.

Sémillon

Sweet white Sauternes, Barsac and Monbazillac owe their rich unction to oaked Sémillon.

This white grape is an enigma. It plays a major role in what most consider the greatest sweet white wine in the world: Château d'Yquem is usually around 80% Sémillon. It's widely travelled. In the early nineteenth century, over 90% of the vines in South Africa were Sémillon, and there are large plantings to this day in Chile, Australia and California. Yet who knows Sémillon? Who can describe its characteristics clearly? Who seeks it out, buys it, loves it? What we can say tentatively are three things. First, that it's a white (whether dry or sweet) of substance: plump and chewy. Second, that it blends well with other varieties, and particularly with Sauvignon Blanc. And third, that it produces excellent results when attacked by noble rot (see page 173).

Its most memorable incarnations are the dry and sweet white wines of Bordeaux and of south-west France (especially Bergerac and Monbazillac). Sweet white Sauternes, Barsac and Monbazillac owe their rich unction to oaked Sémillon, and dry Pessac-Léognan and Bergerac whites owe their linen-like substance, and some of their creaminess, to oaked Sémillon. In Australia's Hunter Valley, the grapes are picked unripe to make a strange, light white wine that is unimpressively neutral when young but which grows in intrigue with age. After that, though, Sémillon seems to perform best as a blending grape, packing and filling in the edges for more overtly characterful varieties … like its old sparring partner Sauvignon Blanc.

Pinot Grigio

Just a hint of apple in Italy, but Pinot Gris is a richer prospect in Alsace.

You'll note I've used the Italian form of this name, and not the French 'Pinot Gris'. The Germans call it Grauburgunder and, when sweet, Rülander; the Hungarians Szürkebarát; Malvoisie is another synonym. So why have I chosen Italian? Because Pinot Grigio is certainly the best-known form of the grape: it's a hugely popular quaffing white from north-east Italy. The success of this crisply neutral white tends to perplex wine waiters. 'It tastes of nothing – and the more it tastes of nothing, the more people like it,' one of them once told me, with a despairing shrug. Was he right? At its best, this grey-pink-berried mutation of Pinot will be smoky, rich, subtly spicy, full of haunting pear or quince fruits and

sometimes ripe summer fruits, too. Flourishing in France's Alsace, it runs to fat, and can end up as the wine world's equivalent of a Danish pastry, though it is also capable of great subtleties and nuance within an always ample frame when yields are tugged back. In Oregon, it is crisper, fresher and more lively, with an orchard-like fruit spectrum lent light and shade by brighter acidity than Alsace generally delivers. It's travelling the world right now, as growers everywhere look to move beyond Chardonnay and Sauvignon in their white-wine production: New Zealand and Argentina have both rolled up their sleeves and got going with it. The litmus test is personality. Is there any?

Gewurztraminer

Scents and sensibility: are you ready to get intimate with Gewurztraminer?

You thought Viognier was scented? Wait until you try Gewurztraminer. There are a few shockingly sensational moments in a wine-drinking life, and the first time you dip your nose into the aromatic embrace of a classically perfumed Gewurztraminer is one of them. Roses and lychees are what most drinkers think of, but ginger and other spices, as well as an entire battery of face creams and skin potions, may also come to mind. Lawrence Alma-Tadema's celebrated painting *The Roses of Heliogabalus* shows a debauched Roman emperor suffocating his dinner-guests in flower petals. That's Gewurztraminer. This pink-skinned variety (its wine is generally golden) is a mutation of

the Tyrolean white variety Traminer, one of the many offspring of grandfather Pinot. Gewurztraminer seems happiest in France's Alsace, where it is the second most widely planted variety, but most wine-producing countries try growing it sooner or later. It's hard to resist. But hard to perfect, too: grown in the wrong places, it can easily seem oily, vegetal, slack or sickly. At its best, Gewurztraminer should be strong and substantial, saturated with perfume from first sniff to final swallow, and capable of conveying mineral complexities in its fiery core. It will never have much acidity, though, and texturally it is rarely as viscous as great Viognier.

Sangiovese

Refinement, complexity, asperity: Sangiovese can be an essay in subtlety and suggestion.

There are challengers to Sangiovese in the quest to find Italy's greatest grape variety, especially Nebbiolo in Piedmont, but most would award the laurels to this late-ripening Tuscan. Tuscan? Actually it's a pan-Italian child: one of its parents is indeed the Tuscan Ciliegiolo, but the other is the southern Calabrese Montenuovo. It has different clonal forms, reflected in its variety of synonyms (Nielluccio, Morellino, Brunello, Prugnolo Gentile) and its customary division into Grosso and Piccolo. Like Chardonnay, its quality range is as vast as that of wine itself. Cheap Sangiovese is pale, thin and acid. Great Sangiovese, by contrast, is a red wine with all the delicacy and refinement of a Renaissance landscape. Midweight, poised and fresh, thanks to its vivid acidity, Sangiovese's range of allusions is diverse and sophisticated (apple, bitter cherry, bay leaf, coffee); its textural presence as supple as fine calfskin; and its food-friendliness and overall digestibility rivals that of good Bordeaux. Chianti Classico, Chianti Rufina, Brunello di Montalcino, Vino Nobile di Montepulciano and some of the 'SuperTuscan' wines now sold under the IGT Toscana name provide the bottles in which to hunt it down, though the variety will often be complemented by blending partners. By contrast, any Italian wine labelled 'Sangiovese' is likely to be simple. It hasn't travelled successfully so far, though great efforts in California may eventually pay off.

Carignan

Like the darkest of storm clouds, Carignan has a sun-silvered side which few of us thought existed.

Carignan is a kind of hangover; not exactly what you want a wine grape to be. Let me explain. Prosperity for Europe's wine growers 50, 70 or 90 years ago meant quantity rather than quality – and Carignan (known as Cariñena or Mazuelo in Spain) will happily produce bunch after bunch of grapes. The wine which those grapes made wasn't particularly becoming; indeed it was often dark, sharp, bitter and acerbic. Plentiful, though, and cheap. Now the world has changed. Few of us want to drink a cheap litre of harsh wine a day. Carignan is being evicted from its old haunts; statistically, it's yesterday's grape. So why am I bothering with it? Simply because, like the darkest of storm clouds, it has a sun-silvered side which few of us thought existed. The climb which reveals this hidden beauty involves persisting with the very oldest plants (100 years or more), and holding Carignan's yields uncompromisingly in check. Do those things, and you can suddenly revel in a red wine which combines density and succulence with an austere yet compelling beauty. Few red grapes can express the mineral quality of Languedoc's finest sites like old-vine Carignan, for example, and it does the same thing in Priorat. Tough love, in this case, works.

Tannat

A rewardingly stern and challengingly craggy wine which combines dark fruits with an inner fire.

The monster. Its very name, like the bright colours of a poisonous caterpillar, warns away the predatory drinker. Yes, Tannat is tannic. Hugely so. When grown in the boulder-strewn clays of Madiran, it produces midnight-black wines which set the mouth throbbing. If you can cope (and food is essential), you will find a rewardingly stern and challengingly craggy wine which combines dark fruits with an inner fire. Oak adds richness, and the wine is already so tannic that a little more from the wood doesn't make much difference; a technique called micro-oxygenation may soften and plump it out (see page 73); decanting for eight hours is always a good idea. It's a wine for winter, for polar explorers, for Christmas Day at the whaling station. Blending it with other grapes like the lighter Cabernet Sauvignon (it's not often you can write that), Cabernet Franc and Fer makes for a slightly easier ride. This monumental curiosity is also grown in the French Basque appellation of Irouléguy (whose cooler conditions give a slightly lighter wine than Madiran), as well as in Côtes de St Mont, in Armagnac country. It has travelled, with Basque emigrants, to Uruguay, where it's the country's most widely planted variety (and locally called Harriague). It makes a solid and bustling red there, though without the almost frightening grandeur it achieves in its distant home under the Pyrenees.

Mourvèdre

Bramble fruits lurk in most ripe Mourvèdre – but so does much else.

Tough, tougher, toughest? Not quite, but almost. This grape is most widely planted in Spain, where it is called Monastrell. In Australia and the USA, it is known as Mataro. Its greatest wines, though, come from Bandol: a sunny amphitheatre of limestone just behind the French Mediterranean naval port of Toulon. It's also grown in the southern Rhône, stiffening spines in Châteauneuf du Pape; it romps across the Languedoc, and spills into Roussillon, too. It reminds me of midnight: dark, quiet, impenetrable, enigmatic … but, at its best, full of strange magic. What was it I found in a 1988 Bandol recently? Rabbit fur and beehives; pine groves on hot hillsides; a garden where *contadini* (Italian smallholders) are preparing tomato paste for the winter; the rosehips which my brothers and I used to dismember in order to make our very own itching powder. That singular wine, admittedly, was old; younger versions major on blackberry fruit, but it usually comes sealed in a treasure chest of tannins, and there is often a kind of brooding quality to it, a sense of unpredictable passions being held in check, under time's lock and key. What the grape always needs is solar force: most of Provence, for example, is simply too cool to grow Mourvèdre. We'll see more of it in the future, I'm sure, when it will no doubt surprise us again.

Grenache

In Spain, it's Garnacha; in Sardinia, it's Cannonau; but around the rest of the world the French form of the name is generally used to describe this sun-loving variety. Sun-loving and tough: it doesn't mind wind; it adores stones and sand; it has a camel's drinking requirements, and can cope with a rainless summer better than most. Its wood is sturdy enough to dispense with stakes and wires and grow like a claw in the open air. And the wine? Strong stuff, too: you won't find many at much under 13.5% or 14%. It's rarely dark in colour, and makes a rosé which often shades away towards orange; its flavours always have a sweet cast to them. Indeed the simplest Grenache wines offer wine drinkers a dip into the jampot. A complex Grenache, by contrast, is as fragrant, sumptuous and profound an expression of sunlight transformed into stone juice as you could hope to find. The tough guy is friendly, too, in that it blends happily with its peers, particularly poised and perfumed Syrah and gutsy, tannic Mourvèdre. This trio is often called GSM in Australia. In France and Spain, its blending partners vary, but Grenache is usually in the thick of most southern blends, especially anything from the extensive pebblefields of the southern Rhône (including star wines Gigondas and Châteauneuf du Pape), from the rocky chaos of Priorat, and from the terraces of southern (Baja) Rioja and Navarra. Sweetly so.

Malbec

What does Malbec have in common with Sauvignon Blanc? It's a prosperous expat. Like Sauvignon Blanc, Malbec's success in the southern hemisphere has very nearly eclipsed its performance back home in France. The grape was carried south in a wave of phylloxera-fuelled emigration at the end of the nineteenth century, and it has since become the signature grape variety for Argentina, where you'll find almost three times as many Malbec vines as in France. Like Sauvignon Blanc in New Zealand (and Shiraz in Australia), Argentine Malbec has a character very much of its own. Dark, vivid, intense, dramatic, vivacious and energetic: great Argentine Malbec comes as close as any wine to evoking the music and dance of the tango. Its fruit character is reminiscent of plums – but sourer, wilder plums than Merlot or Tempranillo can summon (damsons, sloes). The Argentine love of beef may be another reason why it has greater structure and density, and less intrinsic roundness and sweetness, than most Chilean reds. France's Malbec (also known as Côt, Pressac and Auxerrois) is most memorable in Cahors, where it makes a darkly uncompromising, almost ferrous wine with dramatic acid balance and a tannic cape. It blends happily with other varieties, too, and you'll find it playing a supporting role in Bergerac, Buzet, Duras and Fronton, among other wines of the south-west.

Cabernet Franc

Bright, bracing and mouth-freshening: the summer's first raspberries, and a sip of Cabernet Franc.

If the wine world has an *éminence grise*, this is it. Any parent of Cabernet Sauvignon deserves to be called, like the cardinals, an eminence; but what I'm really thinking of is the surreptitious ubiquity with which it has crept around France (where its main aliases are Bouchet, Bouchy or Breton), and now around the wine world. Home is Bordeaux, where it plays a very minor role in support of its grand offspring on the Left Bank, and a rather larger role on the Right: it is usually planted in preference to Cabernet Sauvignon in St Emilion, Pomerol and other nearby appellations. Indeed at Château Cheval Blanc it steps forward into the limelight; the vineyard contains 55% Cabernet Franc vines and only 45% Merlot. Yet the languid, downy, creamy charms of Cheval Blanc are, frankly, untypical of most Cabernet Franc. Far more typical are the wines of the Loire Valley's Chinon, Saumur-Champigny and Bourgueil: pungent, vivid and fresh, with bright raspberry fruits. It has travelled the world most successfully as a blending partner to Cabernet Sauvignon for those seeking to emulate the Bordeaux model, and is now often being reassessed on its own merits as a grape with which to produce structured red wine of sober flavour, but without the sometimes titanic proportions Cabernet can swell to in warm locations. Its great failing is a tendency to smell and taste grassy when grown in too cool a location or with over-high yields.

Nebbiolo

Aged Nebbiolo-based wines have unique gastronomic authority and intrinsic complexity, rolling around the mouth like the sound of gunshot off the hills, scenting the breath like a cachou and stiffening the blood like a national anthem.

Like Pinot Noir, Nebbiolo is difficult. It's difficult for the grower to make it sing. The drinker, too, faces difficulties: bad bottles abound. Like Pinot, its home is a region of limestone hills with four clearly demarcated seasons. Like Pinot, it doesn't much like leaving home. Like Pinot, though, it inspires irrational devotion among those who have seen its light. So what is all the fuss about? A strange combination, in truth, much of which is, again, close to Pinot's appeal: a sometimes pale colour; alluring, almost perfumed scents whose combination of fruits, stones and flowers at best are ethereal; high acidity. Unlike Pinot, though, Nebbiolo matches all this with generous, mouth-puckering tannins, and it is this combination of high acid with high tannin that makes Nebbiolo-based wines such a fearsome challenge for the unwary. The reward (when well aged) are wines of unique gastronomic authority and intrinsic complexity, rolling around the mouth like the sound of gunshot off the hills, scenting the breath like a cachou and stiffening the blood like a national anthem. The chief names are Barolo and Barbaresco, grown on south-facing slopes amid the chaotic and often foggy hills of Piedmont; Spanna and Chiavennasca are synonyms. Other, smaller Nebbiolo-growing areas include Carema and Valtellina. No Nebbiolo grown outside Italy yet remotely resembles that of Piedmont – though Mexico's is enjoyably gutsy.

Gamay

Like white wines, it's best served chilled. That way, all of its intoxicating fruit scents and its slippery gulpability come to the fore.

Gamay is a paradox. Most of the world's most popular grape varieties base their appeal to drinkers on a few Everest wines: wines which are bigger, denser, deeper, richer, more fragrant, more powerful, more intense or more complex than their peers. Gamay doesn't bother with any of that. The only superlative a great Gamay offers the drinker is that of deliciousness. And it does so by being the wine world's closest thing to a hermaphrodite. It's a red wine, in other words, with the weight, structure and balance of a white: high acid, low tannin, bracing poise. Like white wines, it's best served chilled. That way, all of its intoxicating fruit scents and its slippery gulpability come to the fore (as does its ability to accompany

a wide variety of foods well, fish included). The granite soils of northern Beaujolais are where this offspring of Pinot performs best, though the intricacies of France's appellation system mean that you may not see either the word 'Gamay' or the word 'Beaujolais' on its label (instead look for St Amour, Juliénas, Chénas, Moulin-à-Vent, Fleurie, Chiroubles, Morgon, Régnié, Brouilly or Côte de Brouilly). There are other French zones for it, too, on the hills of the Auvergne, in the Loire or in Savoie, though most of these produce light reds best enjoyed in situ. The same is true of Swiss Gamay. Don't let the paradox put you off trying it, though. Delicious can be great, too. (And 'great' wines sometimes forget, alas, to be delicious.)

Tempranillo

Tempranillo brings the strawberries, while American white-oak casks provide the enticing vanilla.

Spain's greatest grape variety has much in common with Italy's Sangiovese. It, too, occurs under a bewildering variety of names (Tinto Fino, Tinta de Toro, Ull de Llebre, Cencibel – and, over the border in Portugal, Tinta Roriz and Aragónez). If you want to taste fine Tempranillo you need to look for other, regional names on Spanish wine labels: Rioja and Ribera del Duero are the most celebrated, but Toro, Navarra and Valdepeñas all provide intriguing variants. And, like Sangiovese, Tempranillo's own character is hard to pin down. Most red grape varieties have an emblematic fruit, and strawberry would be Tempranillo's; one of the secrets of Rioja's enduring appeal is the way that it can, to the casual sniff, recall

strawberries and cream, or strawberries and ice cream. (The ice cream is the legacy of the vanilla-scented American oak in which most Rioja is aged.) Yet grand, dense Tempranillo-based red wine, as produced by the most ambitious growers of Rioja, Ribera del Duero and Toro, is less easy to assign. It is sumptuous, full, sturdy and spicy when young, more plum than strawberry, and ages with assured composure towards a mellow, meaty old age. It is accessible and gratifying; impossible to dislike. Yet to say it had as distinct a character as Cabernet Sauvignon or Pinot Noir would be false. Like Sangiovese, it has been a reluctant traveller so far – except in Portugal, where it helps make great ports and Douro table wines.

The Extended Family

Some key members of the wine vine's extended family.

Aglianico
Dark-skinned, late-ripening variety from the south of Italy, producing richly constituted, firmly structured red wines, especially on the volcanic-soiled slopes of Monte Vulture in Basilicata and in Taurasi in Campania.

Albariño
Perfumed white from rainy Galicia in northern Spain and, as Alvarinho, from Portugal's vinho verde country (the Minho).

Aligoté
A nervy, more acidic white sister grape to Chardonnay in Burgundy (where it is often mixed with blackcurrant liqueur to make a kir). Aligoté is widely grown in Eastern Europe and the nations of the former USSR, too.

Assyrtiko
The white grape behind the piercingly fresh, intensely mineral wines of Santorini, and increasingly widely grown elsewhere in Greece.

Barbera
Intense, energetic and often acidic red Italian variety, making a huge variety of pasta-friendly wines.

Carmenère
An old Bordeaux variety which is widely planted in Chile (and formerly confused with Merlot) as well as Italy (where it was confused with Cabernet Franc). This red grape is dark, soft and voluptuous at best; grassy at worst.

Cinsaut
Sweet, supple and fragrant red-wine grape traditionally used in blends in the south of France, North Africa and the Lebanon. Sometimes spelled Cinsault.

Colombard
Low-character white in California, Australia and South Africa; grassy-fresh in France's Gascony.

Dolcetto
The 'little sweet one' is chiefly used in Piedmont to make deeply coloured, vivacious reds which are less acidic than Barbera and less forbidding in youth than Nebbiolo.

Grüner Veltliner
Amenable Austrian grape variety making dry, peppery whites of some substance. Simple GVs are light and refreshing; ambitious, oaked examples can mimic white burgundy. Great with Asian foods.

Lambrusco
Red grape of central Italy that traditionally made dark, foamy, dry red wine, but is now used to make a wide variety of usually sweet, lightly sparkling and often low-alcohol wines of both colours.

Manseng
Pyrenean grape variety with large (Gros) and small (Petit) variants, producing intensely flavoured dry and sweet white wines with a tropical-fruit flavour spectrum and vivid acidity.

Marsanne
Weighty, languidly scented white variety used in the Rhône Valley (where it is often blended with Roussanne) as well as Australia and California.

Montepulciano
Widely planted Italian red variety, at its best in Marche, Abruzzo, Molise and Puglia, giving deep-flavoured, generous wines. (Not used, though, for Vino Nobile di Montepulciano, which is based on Sangiovese.)

Negroamaro
Southern Italian grape making some of Puglia's best wines (such as Salice Salentino and Copertino): full-flavoured, firm-edged reds with a sweet finish.

Nero d'Avola

Sicily's finest native red variety, making vivacious and characterful reds. Also known as Calabrese.

Palomino

The sherry grape. Makes unexceptional white wine, but transfigured by *flor* (see page 114), fortification and oxidation into improbable grandeur.

Pedro Ximenez

Sherry's sweetening grape, often grown in Montilla. On its own, a black fortified wine resembling syrup of raisins, best poured over ice cream rather than drunk.

Petite Sirah

A name used in California to describe several varieties, most frequently the Rhône crossing Durif (the offspring of true Syrah and the obscure Peloursin). Makes dark, gutsy, forceful, tannic red wines without the polish of Syrah.

Picpoul

Fresh, lemony Languedoc white, once much used for vermouth production.

Pinot Meunier

Red member of the Pinot family, chiefly used as a blending component in Champagne. Its fresh apple fruit helps fill out structured, rooty Pinot Noir and taut, lemony Chardonnay.

Pinotage

South African crossing of Pinot Noir and Cinsaut giving dense, fruity and exuberant reds, sometimes marred by rubbery or estery scents.

Primitivo

See Zinfandel.

Prosecco

White grape of neutral character used for the easy-going sparkling wines of the Venice region.

Roussanne

White grape used in the Rhône (where it is often blended with Marsanne) and Savoie to make wines of aromatic delicacy, hinting at linden or hawthorn. Also grown in Australia and California.

Silvaner

White variety grown in Germany and Alsace (where it is spelled Sylvaner) to make dry, firm, earthy whites of substance and food-friendliness.

Torrontés

Fragrant white variety with a Muscat parent, widely grown in Argentina.

Touriga Nacional

Great indigenous red Portuguese variety producing structured reds in the Douro and Dão, and adding a tea-leaf note to port.

Trebbiano

Widely grown white variety used in France (where it is called Ugni Blanc) for brandy distillation. The Trebbiano family swarms all over Italy, making easy, crisp and neutral white wines of ancient historical pedigree.

Vermentino

Mediterranean white variety (also known as Rolle) producing gentle, fennel-scented whites.

Xinomavro

Grand, late-ripening black variety from northern Greece, producing long-ageing reds of authority and complexity in Naoussa and elsewhere.

Zinfandel

Variety of obscure Croatian origins (where it is called Crljenak Kaštelanski) best known for its success in California – and in southern Italy, too, where it is called Primitivo. Great Californian Zinfandel is a lush, richly fruity, heady red whose brambly and sometimes raisiny fruits can endure for up to a decade. Primitivo in Italy is sweet-fruited, too, though a little stonier and dustier in style. (White Zinfandel, by contrast, is a sweet rosé wine often scented with Muscat or Riesling.)

**PROJECT 7
THE NATURAL
WORLD**

Grape varieties are one reason why wines taste different from one another. In this Project, we tackle a second reason: nature. The French word *terroir* is often used as a synonym for this. Shiraz from the Barossa Valley in Australia contrasts with Syrah from France's Rhône Valley because the geology and climate of those two places are hugely dissimilar. Wine, in other words, is how human beings taste geography.

Vines, grapes and wine flavours are mostly made from two ingredients: sunlight and water.

ABOVE Those sexy gravels have to be Bordeaux, right? Wrong: this is New Zealand's Hawkes Bay.
OPPOSITE Like earthworms, vine roots help create the soil which will eventually nourish them. This promising mixture is in Chile's Maipo Valley.

Earth: Mother and Father

Leaf and fruit are visible to us. What dark adventures, though, are going on beneath the ground?

The life of a vine is very different from yours or mine. We move, incessantly; the vine is still. And it's buried up to its neck in the soil. It's jailed in rock. Its life, from birth to death, is passed in solitary confinement.

The lesson of Europe's greatest winegrowing areas is that the precise circumstances of that stony incarceration matter very much indeed. In Bordeaux, the vineyards of a great property like Château Latour lie next door to the vineyards of modest properties like Châteaux Bellegrave or Fonbadet. In Burgundy, the Grand Cru vineyards of Charmes-Chambertin lie next to vineyards producing simple village wine. In each case, the climate is identical, the grape varieties are identical, and winemaking techniques are similar. There are two major differences. One is the lie of the land: a little more slope here, a little less there. The other

difference is the soilscape underneath the surface: lenses of sand and clay beneath the gravels of Latour, or the precise order in which the layers of limestone, marl and clay have been shuffled in Charmes-Chambertin.

Vines, grapes and wine flavours are mostly made from two ingredients: sunlight and water. Sunlight comes from above; water from below. Nothing about the mineral prison in which vines are locked matters more than drainage. Vines hate soggy roots. One definition of perfect *terroir* would be a soil or rock medium where excess water could quickly drain away, but where the vine could always find a little moisture, even at the end of a long dry summer. That, indeed, seems to be the principal characteristic of the vineyards of Château Latour, which is why it can make a magnificently statuesque wine when conditions are simply too hot and dry for many other Bordeaux vineyards, and why in a rainy vintage its wine still seems to be a little better than its peers. For a vine, the physical characteristics of a soil are more important than the chemical ones.

Truly great vineyard soils occur as rarely as seams of gold. And we're still prospecting.

THIS PAGE Soils have a biography, and you can read it in their strata sequence. The vines will send their roots down through the layers in search of moisture and mineral nutrients. What they find helps create their flavour profile.
OPPOSITE Hurry, everyone: get the grapes in before the water in these clouds over Chablis has a chance to dilute the wine.

Vines, of course, need more than merely water. They need nutrients such as nitrogen, phosphorus and potassium, and they need trace elements: dissolved mineral ions. The roots seek these out, interacting with soil microbes and bacteria as they do so. Exactly what vine roots are doing as they rummage and thrust underground is not yet fully understood. We cannot prove that the roots of old vines, wandering 15 or 20 metres underground through fractured, fissured or friable rock of a particular chemical composition, leave a flavoury trace in the wine and even an aromatic architecture – but the experience of generations of wine tasters and drinkers suggests that it does.

So what do we know with certainty? In terms of soil nutrition, less is more. Well-fed vines produce a uselessly leafy plant, or an over-large crop of tasteless grapes. That's why the rich, deep loams so favoured for most agricultural crops in general make poor vineyards. A stony vineyard tends to produce better wine from leaner vines.

We also understand that soils need to be healthy, too. In particular, excessive chemical fertilizers, pesticides and herbicides have a destructive, sterilizing effect on soils, and the use of heavy machinery has a negative impact by compacting those soils, too. A healthy vineyard soil is one that is physically worked as the seasons turn, which encourages the roots to penetrate deeply into it, and which has a high level of microbial and bacteriological life within it.

There is, though, no simple geological formula for great wine. Wine is not oil. Outstanding wine can come from an extraordinary variety of rock and soil types of various geological ages. The grapes that

make Champagne, Cognac and sherry, for example, are in large part grown on chalk. Limestone is characteristic of Burgundy, St Emilion, Chianti and Coonawarra in Australia. Beaujolais and the northern Rhône are dominated by granite, as are many South American vineyards; the Douro Valley, where port is made, is a sea of rocky schist; slate slides off some of Germany's finest vineyards; there are great vineyards on sandy soils in the southern Rhône Valley and in Australia's McLaren Vale; volcanic ash and pumice on the Greek island of Santorini produce sensational wines. The vineyards of Bordeaux's Médoc area are, in these terms, a jumble: they are composed of millions of stones of diverse origin rolled down by rivers from the mountains of the Pyrenees and central France. In this case, it is not so much the chemistry of the stone which matters as its physical presence, in the form of deep gravel banks. Yet the more you study the gravel, the more you realize that the difference between one vineyard and another is the non-gravelly deposits within it. Much of Châteauneuf du Pape is similar.

What all of these different vineyard sites do have in common, though, is that they are neither too fertile nor totally lacking in nutrients; that the upper-layer drainage and lower-layer water retention are both good, and that they have adequate friability to allow the roots to penetrate deeply within.

It's not hard to find good vineyard soils, especially if you are prepared to use irrigation to replace rainfall deficiencies. The earth is a generous mother, and the vine is an undemanding child. Truly great vineyard soils, though, occur as rarely as seams of gold. And we're still prospecting.

Sky: A Life Lived

In the life of a vine, adventure comes from above.
Its biography is a long meteorological saga.

Vines, we know, are imprisoned from birth to death.
They cannot move. They never miss a dawn; they never
doze through dusk. They take whatever nature throws
at them. And, even in the sweetest of climates, that
makes them heroically hardy. Dark hours of winter
frost; lashing rain as the seasons turn; daily exposure
to glaring sunlight and heat over a long summer: vines
can withstand conditions from which mammals must
imperatively seek shelter. So, too, do pomegranate trees.
And plum trees, and apples. The vine, surely, is no different
from other members of the fruit world?

On the contrary: it is very different. This is why the
concept of the 'vintage' is supremely important in the wine
world, but almost irrelevant (quantity aside) to other fruit
crops. The vine has the uncanny ability to register almost
everything that happens to it during a season. Once it has
been through fermentation, you or I can taste those subtle
differences in the weather pattern. Why does burgundy from
2005 taste better than burgundy from 2004? Because the
weather was sunnier and drier. That, too, is why Latour 2003
is twice the price of Latour 2002. That is why a bottle of
Barolo from 1978 would be opened with a sense of keen
anticipation, but why a bottle of Barolo from 1977 would be
opened with great nervousness. A vintage represents the
sum total of all the weather conditions experienced by the
vine in a particular year. Great vintages taste rich, articulate,

profound; poor vintages taste sharp and hard. Great vintages endure; poor vintages die soon.

There's more, though. A few pages ago, we learned that it is the interplay of natural conditions (soil, slope, sky) which accounts for many of the most fundamental differences between wines, and which are often referred to by the French word *terroir*. Within well-established fine-wine regions (like Bordeaux or Burgundy), it is generally soil that distinguishes great-wine sites from more modest achievers. But in newer winegrowing environments, or when you come to compare one region with another a great distance away, climate is far more important than soil. If Syrah from Hermitage in the Rhône Valley tastes as different as it does from Shiraz from the Barossa Valley, climate is the main cause. *Terroir* is a very complicated equation … but climate is the most important part of that equation.

The way in which both climate (the long-term pattern) and weather (the day to day departures from that pattern) leave their print on wines is as subtle as a marine cloudscape. Most grape varieties have fundamental temperature requirements. Some need less sunshine and warmth to ripen fully (such as Pinot Noir among reds and Sauvignon Blanc among whites); others need more (Mourvèdre and Muscat). A little wind is often beneficial; a lot of wind is always destructive. Wet winters, and small amounts of rain during the growing season, are usually welcome; harvest rain is always unwelcome. Spring frosts and summer hail are perennial hazards. After that, though, many varieties prove surprisingly adaptable. Some wine regions have maritime climates

(characterized by mild winters and warm summers, with little day-night termperature variation) while others have a continental climate pattern (with cold winters and hot summers, and sometimes a large day-night variation). One would expect the two patterns to favour different varieties. Yet Cabernet Sauvignon and Merlot, for example, flourish both in maritime Bordeaux and in continental Washington State, though the wines produced in each location are very different. Syrah/Shiraz generally thrives in continental climates – yet magnificent Syrah wines are produced within a stone's throw of the Mediterranean in Languedoc's La Clape, and next to the Gulf of St Vincent in McLaren Vale.

Let's indulge in a little dangerous summary, though. It's generally true to say that any particular variety generally performs best when it saunters rather than races towards ripeness, and that the best vintages in those marginal or semi-marginal conditions are generally the hotter ones. I personally believe (though others disagree) that the greatest still wines will generally come from fruit whose juice needs no additions or subtractions in the winery. From fruit, in other words, where nature has provided an ideal level and balance of sugar and acidity. 'My work with 2005,' says Burgundian winemaker Sylvain Pitiot of Clos de Tart, remembering the beauty of that summer's weather pattern, 'is nothing. I'm serious. All the work was made by the *terroir* and by nature.' It is an irony of winemaking life that the most struggle and effort usually goes into the worst vintages, or making tasty wine from the least suitable sites.

The way in which both climate and weather leave their print on wines is as subtle as a marine cloudscape.

OPPOSITE An unsettled late spring evening in Corbières. Those vines could do with a little rain to set against the fierce days to come.

FACT FILE:
The Natural World

Vine food Light, water and trace elements. Over 80% of plant matter is derived from CO_2 via photosynthesis.

Ideal soil conditions
Free-draining, healthy, biologically and microbially rich though nutritionally poor topsoils over moisture-retaining subsoils. Vines grow well in a wide variety of specific soil and rock types, though a neutral or high pH is generally preferable to a very low one.

Ideal climate conditions
Varies by grape variety, but warm enough to achieve ripeness over the full length of an average season. Unripe or overripe characters are undesirable; rapid ripening rarely delivers complex aromas or flavours.

Nature's worst tricks
Spring frosts, high winds or heavy rains at flowering time, hailstorms or heavy rain in summer, rain at harvest time.

**PROJECT 8
THE HUMAN ROLE**

Left to its own devices, every wine would finish as vinegar. The human role in wine production is, thus, vital. For inexpensive branded wines, it is all-important: aroma and flavour in such wines are chiefly created by winemaking and blending strategies. In expensive fine wines, the winemaker works in partnership with nature – to allow the potential uniqueness of a site to emerge with maximum articulacy.

Gardening: The Vineyard

Ask any serious winemaker, and they will all say the same thing. If you don't grow great grapes first, you can't then make great wine.

These are the most important four pages in this book. Winemaking is nurture: superintending, fashioning, refining. Vineyard work, by contrast, is an engagement with nature itself. The vineyard (vine, stone, sky) constitutes the genome of every wine, and by working in it and studying it, ideally over a lifetime, winegrowers can come to understand it and maximize its potential. It is in the stone walls of the vineyard, rather than the stainless-steel tanks of the winery, that you'll find the tiny door that opens onto great wine.

Let's state the obvious: not all vineyards are born equal, just as not all human babies born in the next 20 minutes have the potential to teach mathematics at Cambridge. Exactly what one does in a vineyard depends on its potential. Treating

vineyards in Australia's Riverland or California's Central Valley in the same way as the best vineyards in Burgundy would be pointless, since these vineyards are incapable of delivering the quality which you can obtain from Bonnes Mares or Montrachet. Slapdash viticulture in great vineyards, by contrast, is a morally criminal act. It denies a rare patch of earth the chance to speak with the articulacy of which it is capable.

Once a vineyard is planted, there are two fundamental actions every winegrower undertakes every year. After harvest, the vines must be pruned and its annual growth cut and cleared. (The vine, remember, was designed to climb trees. Unpruned, it will soon fill a field with a chaotic tangle of canes, shoots and tendrils.)

Come winter's end, the vine will recommence its growth. It will flower, shyly enough, in early summer, and needs no human or insect help to pollinate its flowers. A light breeze will do; the fruit will set, and later swell and ripen of its own accord.

There is no more important viticultural judgement than deciding when to pick. The later you leave it, the greater the risks.

ABOVE A bonny bunch ... though the yields may be a bit too high to produce a concentrated wine.
OPPOSITE No machine duplicates the care and gentleness of hand-harvesting. The world's finest grapes are still hand-picked.

Humans, though, are necessary to harvest the grapes. Both pruning and harvesting can now be done mechanically. Few, if any, vineyards will actually see nothing but a machine rattle twice yearly through them, but that is the theoretical minimum.

Most vines are now trained onto a wine trellis, and the exact way in which the parts of the vine (trunk, shoots and bunches) are positioned against that trellis has been found to be hugely significant. Vines can, though, stand unaided if pruned in the right way. These are generally called 'bush vines'. In bare winter, they look like claws emerging from the earth, and in summer … like little bushes. Controlling the size of the crop is the key quality decision every winegrower must make. What's the equation? Fewer grapes will provide more concentration of flavour – but you'll have less wine to sell. More grapes means more wine, but more dilution, too.

Irrigation is vital for some vineyards. It's usually banned in Europe (to lessen over-production; Europe's natural rainfall patterns are currently adequate for a vine's needs) but essential for most southern-hemisphere vineyards. Both fertilization and irrigation need a light touch. When it comes to its own food and drink requirements, the vine is more camel than pig.

So much for the basics. What about the best? I've called this section 'Gardening' for the simple reason that those growing the best grapes in the world more closely resemble gardeners than farmers. They will physically work the soil in the winter, fertilize it sparsely with natural composts, and avoid heavy machinery of any sort: the aim is to maximize the microbial life in the soil, and to keep its physical structure light and airy so that the roots can penetrate deeply into it. They will usually grow grass or companion crops between the rows to act as green fertilizer; when weeds need removing, this will be done by physical rather than chemical means.

Yields will be kept low by hard winter pruning, and sometimes by summer pruning of bunches, too. The vines will be as densely planted as possible to ensure deep root growth and low individual production. At the same time, the canopy of leaves will be trimmed and trained to ensure that the bunches that remain receive a perfection of sunlight, and have enough air movement to keep rot at bay. Any vine which grows profuse vegetation is wasting its energy.

There is no more important viticultural judgement than deciding when to pick. The later you leave it, the greater the risks. The consequence of this was that, in the past, many wines were made from grapes picked prematurely. Picking at full ripeness is, today, thought worth the risk: unripe flavours jar, whereas ripe ones gratify.

The most recent revolution stands halfway between winegrowing and winemaking. Fastidious hand-picking of the grapes into small boxes avoids the premature crushing they used to receive in large hoppers and trailers. The subsequent sorting of the fruit on vibrating tables, and later by hand, means that only perfect berries drop (by gravity) into the fermentation vat. This super-selectivity has brought a new density and sumptuousness to the world's greatest wines.

Everything I have written above, though, implies a sweet summer. Alas, few are. Like doctors, winegrowers find their greatest efforts go not into maximizing the good health and good fortune of those in their care, but into minimizing the effects of disaster. A spring frost, rain and high winds at flowering time, a vicious hailstorm towards the end of the ripening period, followed by heavy harvest rain: this is the nightmare scenario. It can double the annual workload – for, at best, a reduced crop of grapes whose quality will be necessarily compromised. A winegrower's lot is not always a happy one.

OPPOSITE ABOVE LEFT Yes, the nets cost a lot – but losing the grapes to the birds would cost even more.

OPPOSITE ABOVE CENTRE His cellphone will have changed by now, but the design of the pruning scissors has long been perfected.

OPPOSITE ABOVE RIGHT These open-air heaters at Château Montelena are ready for forecasts of frost on spring nights in Napa.

OPPOSITE BELOW These Cabernet vines are desperate for an autumn drink, but the small, healthy grapes bode well for the wine to come.

Cooking: The Winery

Is wine magic? It is – though the magician is nature. The job of the winemaker, like that of the midwife, is to understand the natural process he or she is overseeing, and to intervene when and where necessary to ensure the best outcome for both mother (the human enterprise) and child (the wine).

If nature hasn't delivered the raw materials you require, you can make adjustments.

Winemaking, like writing poems, blending perfumes or bringing up children, is a simple action overlain with many complications. Let's start with its simple side. The only prior knowledge you will need is an understanding of alcoholic fermentation: the conversion of sugar by microorganisms called yeasts into equal quantities of alcohol and carbon dioxide.

White wine is usually made from white (or, more accurately, green) grapes. They are crushed to express their juice, and that juice is then settled. The clarified juice ferments, using the yeasts naturally present on the grape skins and in the air. After fermentation, the yeast remains are deposited and the new wine run off into a clean container. It contains no more sugar, so can ferment no further. It is drunk – or bottled.

Red wine always requires red or black grapes. Since, a few rare exceptions aside, the colouring matter lies in the skins and not in the transparent juice, the grapes ferment and then macerate together with their skins. This takes, typically, two to three weeks. When fermentation, colour extraction and tannin extraction are over, the wine is run off (and the skins pressed) into a clean container before, once again, being drunk or bottled.

Pink or rosé wine is usually created by macerating red grape skins with grape juice overnight or for a day or two, though it can also result from mixing red and white wine.

Sparkling wine is begun in the same way as white wine. After fermentation is complete, more sugar and yeast is added, and the wine is bottled and sealed. A second fermentation occurs – though this time, the carbon dioxide produced cannot escape. The wine becomes pregnant with gas. The sediment is swiftly removed and the wine resealed without allowing the CO_2 to escape. When finally opened, the wine fizzes with all that dissolved gas – and the laughter rings out.

What about fortified wines like sherry, port and Madeira? If you add high-strength alcohol to partially fermented wine or grape juice, it will stop (or refuse to begin) fermenting, since yeasts cannot survive when the alcohol level in a liquid passes about 17% by volume. The natural, grape-given sweetness of the juice or part-fermented wine will be thus preserved.

Those are the basics: the winemaking equivalent of how to make an omelette, bake a loaf of bread, or roast a joint of meat. Here's a quick guide to the commoner complications.

ABOVE The waiting room: metamorphosis beckons. The final verdict on quality is still years away, though.

OPPOSITE ABOVE LEFT Winemaking produces a greenhouse gas: here comes the CO_2.

OPPOSITE ABOVE CENTRE The last stage of barrel-making is to toast the inside of the staves: another flavour note.

OPPOSITE ABOVE RIGHT Job (almost) done. There are just under 300 bottles of wine in each barrel.

OPPOSITE BELOW Ancient and messy, but some winemakers still think the basket press is best for extracting those final drops.

If nature hasn't delivered the raw materials you require, you can make adjustments. Adding sugar will raise the final alcohol levels (often needed in cool regions); adding acid will give the wine more of an edge (often needed in hotter ones). You can also add enzymes, tannins and assorted chemical compounds (of which sulphur is the commonest and most necessary). You can remove alcohol, too; indeed you can even remove water.

The vessels in which fermentation takes place are, most commonly, stainless steel, concrete, small new oak casks or large older oak vats: each gives a different result. Many ambitious white wines, for example, are fermented in small oak casks; and most fine red wines are aged after fermentation in similar casks. The age of the wood is significant (new wood delivers most aroma and flavour); so is its origin, and in particular whether that oak is pedunculate (*Quercus robur*) and usually of French origin, or white (*Quercus alba*) and usually of American origin. White oak gives sweet aromas and flavours: vanilla and even coconut are typical, and it can sometimes add an almost minty scent to Shiraz. French or European pedunculate oak smells and tastes less obviously vanillic; it can suggest toast, coffee or cedar.

The force (or gentleness) with which winemaking operations are carried out has major flavour implications, as does the temperature at which they take place. Many red wines are given a 'cold soak' before fermentation, to intensify fruit flavours; white wines, too, can undergo skin maceration before fermentation to add perfume. Great sparkling wine needs very gentle, slow

pressing of the juice, and cool fermentation; vigorous, warm extraction and extended maceration of red wines results in dark, heavy, tannic wines. The skins floating in vats of fermenting red wine form a hard, dry cap on the surface of the wine, and this must be moistened and washed by the fermenting juice: the exact way in which this is done affects wine styles, too. Red burgundy is gently 'punched' down; vintage port needs a more energetic approach. All red wines and some whites undergo something called malolactic fermentation, 'malo' or MLF: this is a bacteriological conversion of 'appley' malic acid into 'milky' lactic acid. Whether or not you allow a white wine to undergo this, and how and in what container you oversee it for a red, is another flavoury subtlety.

All wines, too, need regular freshening with a little oxygen prior to bottling. The classic way of carrying this out is by racking, which means moving wine from one container to another; a newer way, though, is via micro-oxygenation – the trickling of small streams of oxygen through the wine. If wines are stored for an extended period on their yeast lees (the deposit left after fermentation), those lees add body, volume and glossiness to them. Sometimes the lees are 'beaten' or agitated to increase this effect. Wines may also be both fined and filtered before bottling.

Lots of possibilities, as you see. But is the baby beautiful?

ABOVE The rear end of a large steel tank. Gravity will empty this one; in the old days, everything had to be forked out by hand.
OPPOSITE Supremely neutral and clean, the virtue of steel is to let the fruit flavours sing out unsullied. The wines need air, though, to keep them fresh.

The vessels in which fermentation takes place are, most commonly, stainless steel, concrete, small new oak casks or large older oak vats: each gives a different result.

FACT FILE:
The Human Role

Major vineyard decisions
Crop size (decided by pruning); ripeness (decided by timing of picking); post-harvest handling.

Major white-winemaking decisions Speed of pressing; type and temperature of container used for fermentation; contact with yeast lees; MLF; moment and circumstances of bottling.

Major red-winemaking decisions Cold soak; extraction and maceration method and temperature; type of container used for fermentation and ageing; type of oxygenation and use of lees; moment and circumstances of bottling.

THE JOURNEY

The decision to travel, now that the age of climate-change innocence is over, has become complicated: personal pleasure means planetary poison. Wine, as we've discovered, gives us the chance to smell and taste other places on earth. In this, the final part of the book, we're going to put the theoretical knowledge we've acquired so far into practical use. We're going to travel – by taste. You don't need a passport, inoculations, a phrase book or carbon offsets. Sniff the sweet scrub of Languedoc, sip the cascading light that bathes New Zealand's roomy landscapes and digest the mineral solitude of the Médoc's deep gravel banks without leaving your kitchen. All you need is sensual curiosity and an open mind.

**PROJECT 9
READING
THE MAP**

Our journey is no different from any other in one respect: a little equipment is useful. That equipment helps us make sense of the vast range of undifferentiated tastes and flavours offered by the wine world. Some of it is provided by wine producers: names, dates and other labelling information. Wine maps make the fragments cohere.

Maps

Maps matter because they explain the intricate logic of some European wine regions.

ABOVE The Douro Valley even makes for a map of high drama. See what the fuss is about on page 157.

Great bottles come first, of course – but maps are next. The detailed cartography in Hugh Johnson's *The World Atlas of Wine*, now co-authored by Jancis Robinson, makes it the single most useful reference book any wine enthusiast can own. Why do maps matter so much?

First, maps matter because they help organize our lives. Where is Champagne in relation to Paris? Is San Francisco more of a wine town than Los Angeles? Is Sydney the best place to stay if you want to visit the Barossa Valley? A glance at a map will steer you. (East, yes and no, by the way, are the answers to those three questions.)

Secondly, maps matter because they explain the intricate logic of some European wine regions. Burgundy is the classic example. It might seem puzzling that vineyards above the little village of Vosne-Romanée make some of the most expensive bottles of wine in the world whereas

vineyards a few hundred metres beneath the village are sold simply as 'Burgundy' (Bourgogne) at less than a tenth of the price. Follow the lines of relief on a map, and the puzzle will begin to make sense.

With a little experience, you will soon be able to use maps to help explain what you are tasting. Why, for example, does Gigondas seem brisker, tighter and tauter than soft and meaty Châteauneuf du Pape, just a few miles away? The map will show you that the position of a mountain chain called the Dentelles de Montmirail means that much of Gigondas faces north, evading the sun's fiercest rays, whereas Châteauneuf is an undulating, stony plateau far from the high hills, where the solar force is unmitigated. Why does the soft strawberry and vanilla of Tempranillo in Rioja turn to fresher cherry and chocolate in nearby Ribera del Duero? Look at the lines of relief. Much of Rioja lies at 450 metres above sea level; Ribera del Duero is twice as high. That means that the nights are cooler – preserving acidity and tightening fruit character.

Labels

Labels are the wine drinker's best friend – though they can sometimes seem like an enemy.

There are two sorts of label: front labels, which contain all the 'official' information a wine producer is legally obliged to supply; and back labels, which are optional and which can communicate almost anything. Sometimes, mischievous producers reverse their roles, so that the 'official information' appears to be on the back of the bottle and something far simpler and more graphic is on the front. The law bites its lip. More often, regrettably, back labels are omitted altogether.

Alcoholic strength (8.5–16% abv for most unfortified wines, with 13.5% being typical today) and producer's name: both of these are useful pieces of front-label information. So, too, are vintages, and the name of the overall region from which the wine comes. Mention of the wine's variety or varieties, wherever given, is always helpful. Many European wines, though, will specify the

name of an obscure growing region and vineyard, yet fail to mention the grape variety or varieties. What does one expect from a bottle of Coteaux du Vendômois, Squinzano or Ribera del Guadiana? It's hard for most of us to say. Not every drinker, after all, knows that Chablis is always 100% Chardonnay or that Sancerre is 100% Sauvignon Blanc. If we don't know this about famous wines, what chance do we have with the rarer ones?

This is why back labels are so important. Not only can they provide the drinker-friendly information which official regulations fail to elicit, such as information about grape varieties and oak handling, but they can also tell the story of a wine. No wine producer should deprive their wine of a back label.

ABOVE LEFT AND CENTRE Southern hemisphere wine labels beat the north for simplicity, if not elegance. At least German wines, unlike French, cite the variety. ABOVE RIGHT Back label and 'official' front label in one – allowing a little eye-seduction on the other side. RIGHT Typefaces, colours and designs are all culture-specific: you know at a glance you're in California.

Back labels are important. Not only can they provide the drinker-friendly information which official regulations fail to elicit, but they can also tell the story of a wine.

Names

I won't deceive you. Names are an obstacle along the path to wine knowledge.

Brand names; names of grape varieties, regions, appellations (and their non-French equivalents), vineyards and producers; even the words for old vines, harvesting techniques, particular blends, local quality hierarchies or winemaking stratagems: there will be hundreds of thousands of these, in a dozen or more different languages. The one certainty is that no one knows all of them; most of us, 'experts' included, jog along with partial knowledge. I've given up worrying about this. So, I'd suggest, should you, especially in the internet age, with its helpful search engines.

It's useful, though, to distinguish between the different categories of name. Wherever you see the ™ or ® symbols, you know that a name is a brand rather than an appellation, a vineyard or a variety; most of us, too, are able to spot proper names, even without the usual signpost words like 'Château', 'Domaine', 'Bodega' and so on. Grape varieties, increasingly, will either be familiar, or if unfamiliar be listed or explained on the back label. The rest is often geographical information of some sort. Pursue it (in books or on the internet) as far as your interest takes you.

Try to feel at ease with names, though, even if you don't understand every one. Every new bottle brings meaning. Some names will become warmly precious – 'your' wine. I think of Madiran like that, and Bandol, and unfortified wine from the Douro; if I was rich enough, it would be Pomerol and the Grands Crus Classés of St Emilion. You may come to view other names as treacherous. The glossary at the end of this book, and many of the names we are about to enounter on our great journey, will get you started.

LEFT St Emilion is one of my favourite wines – but there are still names in the area which are new to me.

Dates

Most wines go to market clutching their birth certificate. No two vintages are ever alike. Knowing a little bit about the quality of recent vintages in major wine regions, therefore, is very useful.

How do you acquire this knowledge? By trying as many wines as possible. There are shortcuts: vintage charts, which rate the quality of vintages, by region, with a numerical score. Many are available on the internet; you will find them, too, in wine books.

They are more useful for northerly regions in the northern hemisphere and southerly ones in the southern hemisphere, since it is in these locations that wines show the greatest variation between vintages. No region is immune to vintage variation, though. Hot, dry vintages tend to create big wines with warmth and richness, and win higher scores; cooler or wetter vintages create slimmer, fresher but sometimes sharper wines, and tend to be given lower scores.

Don't, however, become hypnotised by charts. The differences between vintages, especially when the wines are young, are sometimes better viewed as stylistic rather than qualitative, and you may find you prefer the wines of a cooler year to those of a hot one, even though they won't last as long in the cellar. Winemaking techniques mean that few truly bad wines reach export markets, even from difficult vintages.

The greatest and most enduring wines of all, though, will always come from truly fine vintages, when nature was uncomplicatedly generous. If you are going to buy fine wine to store for a decade or more, therefore, you should always consult a vintage chart.

ABOVE The older the vintage, the more fussy you should be; most wines are enjoyable young, but only the best vintages endure.

No two vintages are ever alike. Knowing a little bit about the quality of recent vintages, therefore, is very useful.

FACT FILE:
Reading the Map

Maps From simple details of location to profound insights into why wines taste as they do, maps have no substitute as a source of information for wine lovers.

Labels A wine's label is, for the browsing shopper, its life story. Some are generous with the detail; others, alas, are mean. Learning how to find your way around a label will help you to get the most out of every bottle.

Names The mental air in the wine world is thick with a blizzard of names. Don't be put off. Work slowly, letting the names acquire meaning as you try more wines.

Dates More important in cooler-climate zones than in reliably warm ones. Follow the great vintages if you can, since they provide wine's reference points. Don't, though, ignore lesser vintages, since they provide plenty of pleasure too.

VINTAGES: THE BARE BONES

Most summers fall somewhere between these two extremes of vintage heaven and vintage hell.

GOOD VINTAGES	BAD VINTAGES
Wet winter	Dry winter
Cool early spring	Warm early spring
Fine late spring	Spring frosts
Dry, still weather for flowering	Wet, windy weather for flowering
Warm, dry summer	Cool, damp summer
Occasional showers	Hailstorms
Hot, dry summer's end	Wet, humid summer's end
Dry, fine harvest weather	Harvest rain

PROJECT 10
PLACES: France

Geologically youthful, agriculturally well-endowed, its landmass melding an Atlantic west to a Mediterranean south and an Alpine east, France's natural aptitude for winegrowing diversity is complemented by the restless sensual curiosity of her people. In contrast to Italy, however, vine-growing is by no means ubiquitous in France. Specialisms and singularities abound. That's why French wine is such fun to explore.

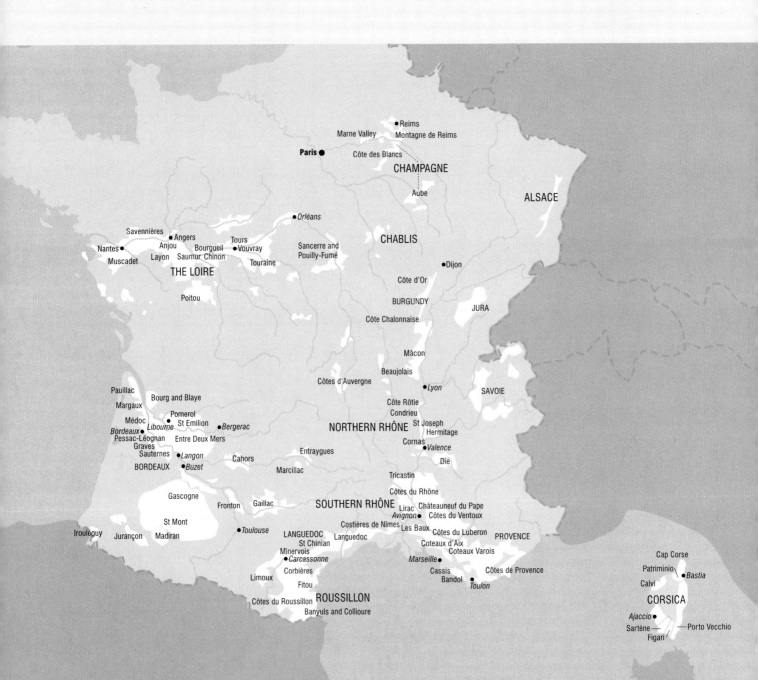

Bordeaux

Bordeaux lies in south-west France. Its name means 'waterside' or 'seaside'. As that name suggests, Bordeaux is a land of open skies, languid rivers and one vast estuary, the Gironde, which empties into the Atlantic past vine-covered gravel banks dumped during the Ice Ages and their watery intermissions.

The most important grape variety in Bordeaux is Merlot. Next, in the hotter spots only, comes Cabernet Sauvignon. Cabernet Franc is used to blend with both, adding complexity of flavour. Bordeaux's climate is one of typical seaside gentleness: long, warm, luminous summers shading into mild autumns. The Atlantic is a moody sea, though, and rain clouds can come romping in at any time.

These grapes and this climate combine to create red wines that provide a world benchmark: lithe, appetizing, refreshing, satisfying, digestible and harmonious. Those grown on what is known as the Left Bank of the Gironde (in places like the Pauillac, St Julien and Margaux areas of the Médoc) tend to be dominated by the blackcurranty freshness and vigour of Cabernet Sauvignon. Those grown on the Right Bank of the Gironde (in places like St Emilion and Pomerol) tend to be softer, fuller and plummier, thanks to a higher percentage of Merlot. Good red Bordeaux ages as well as any wine on earth, acquiring harmony, fragrance and composure with each year that passes.

Bordeaux means white wine, too. Its inexpensive dry wines (often called Bordeaux or Entre-Deux-Mers) are fresh, leafy and light. More money should fill your glass with something sumptuous and creamy (look out for white Pessac-Léognan). Both partner food well.

Bordeaux's sweet wines, the best of them from the AOCs of Sauternes or Barsac, are richly layered, lush and glycerous, balanced as much by the plump legacy of oak casks and the tang of botrytis-affected grapes as by acidity. The grape varieties used for both dry and sweet wines are principally Sémillon and Sauvignon Blanc – but varietal character gives way, here, to the taste of place and local winemaking traditions.

OPPOSITE This is Château Lynch-Moussas in Pauillac, and a generous Cabernet harvest is beckoning. If the leaves are still green, it's because of clay lenses hidden deep in the gravels.

TRY Compare an inexpensive red Bordeaux with a similarly priced Cabernet-Merlot from Australia, New Zealand, Washington State or South Africa. Which is better on its own? And with food?

TRY Compare a bottle of red from the Pauillac AOC with one from the Pomerol AOC (expensive). Look for density, texture and meaty blackcurrant flavours in the Pauillac, which will be dominated by Cabernet Sauvignon. The Merlot-dominated Pomerol should be smoother and rounder, with flavours of plum and perhaps a sweet creaminess, too.

TRY Compare an inexpensive dry white Bordeaux made principally from Sauvignon Blanc with a Loire Sauvignon de Touraine. The Bordeaux will probably be a little softer and fuller than the Loire.

TRY A Sauternes and compare it with a sweet Jurançon from south-west France. Sauternes is usually made with botrytis-affected grapes, Jurançon with sun- and wind-shrivelled grapes: can you taste that difference?

WHAT PEOPLE LOVE ABOUT

Red Bordeaux
+ Its mid-weight balance.
+ Its warm, often cedary scent.
+ Its subtle mixture of fruit, oak and stone flavours.
+ Its digestibility.
+ Its ability to age into a softer, mellower wine with time.

Barsac and Sauternes
+ Their textural unctuousness.
+ Their rich, almost fatty scents and flavours.
+ Their lush summer fruits.

Burgundy, Jura and Savoie

Greater Burgundy encompasses five regions. Furthest north lies Chablis. This is where the world's freshest and most mouthwatering Chardonnays come into being: green-gold, sour-ripe whites grown on fossil oyster shells whose stony austerity can blossom, with time, into a strange, maternal richness.

Next comes the Côte d'Or, the 'golden slope': Burgundy's heartland. The Côte de Nuits, between Nuits-St Georges and Dijon, is home to the world's greatest light-bodied reds, made from Pinot Noir: mostly clear, fresh and frank, but occasionally flowering into wines of astonishing perfume and fruit presence. The Côte de Beaune further south breeds reds of greater variability (from chunky Pommard to slender Santenay) – and a few of the world's greatest Chardonnay-based white wines. The depth, grandeur and substance of Montrachet and the stony succulence of Meursault are two highlights. Never expect consistency here, though, even among the top wines (labelled

Premier Cru or with a separate, Grand Cru appellation of their own). The Côte d'Or has 'disappointment' tattooed on its bottom.

The Côte Chalonnaise is a small region of red-wine understudies and white-wine bridesmaids. They offer appealing value but seldom soar like the best of the Côte d'Or.

The much bigger Mâconnais, by contrast, is full of soft, comely Chardonnay which rarely disappoints. If you want to understand the character and attraction of the world's most celebrated white grape variety, start here.

Finally, in Beaujolais, we meet a new grape: Gamay. We find a new soil type, too. The limestones typical further north give way to granite. The resulting red wine remains light, but the granite brings a hard, glittering quality which, combined with the juiciness of Gamay, makes a wine of spirit-lifting drinkability and gulpability. Serve it cool.

Burgundy is more name-packed than any wine region on earth, and tracking the names isn't easy. The best Beaujolais may be labelled 'Morgon', 'Moulin-à-Vent' or one of eight local names, with no mention on the bottle of 'Beaujolais'. A reference book will help you decode the nomenclature – and steer you to two tiny regions lying east of Burgundy: Jura (pale reds and tangy whites) and Savoie (whose fresh and delicate wines of both colours are mostly consumed locally).

OPPOSITE Not a typical Burgundian scene: this is Chiroubles, in Beaujolais – and yes, the Rhône isn't far away. Untrellised bush vines hint at the south.

TRY A plain Chablis from a reliable producer against a good Mâcon white, such as St Véran or Viré-Clessé. Note the Chablis' mouth-freshening sourness against the softer, richer, lemon-cream style of the Mâcon wine.

TRY A red Gevrey-Chambertin from the Côte de Nuits against a red Beaune from the Côte de Beaune – then compare both with a New Zealand Pinot Noir from Martinborough or Central Otago. The Beaune should be the most delicate, the Gevrey Chambertin more forthright and firm. The New Zealand Pinot will be deepest and fruitiest – but it may be less subtle.

TRY A Beaujolais-Villages or a cru Beaujolais, and compare it with a Fronton from south-west France or a Tarrango from Australia. See if you like them better served cool than at room temperature.

WHAT PEOPLE LOVE ABOUT

Red Burgundy
+ Its lightness, zest and energy.
+ Its perfumes and flavours of cherry and raspberry.
+ Its finesse – and its inner fire.

White Burgundy
+ Its stylistic range, from stony Chablis to plump Pouilly-Fuissé.
+ Its vinosity or 'winey' quality.
+ Its ability, with age, to acquire banquet-like dimensions.
+ Its subtlety and ability to nourish.

Beaujolais
+ Its fresh, sweetly fruity scents.
+ Its brisk and juicy flavours.
+ Its cheerful gulpability.
+ Its deliciousness when chilled.

Champagne

TRY A Blanc de Blancs Champagne against a Blanc de Noirs Champagne: note the lemony finesse of the former and the deep, structured apple or green plum fruit of the latter.

TRY A big-brand Champagne (like Moët or Pommery) against a grower's Champagne: notice the easy-going, gentle and affable nature of the former against the more marked personality and character of the latter.

TRY A pink (rosé) Champagne, and look for the typical strawberry notes which come from adding a little red Pinot Noir wine to a typical Champagne blend (this is how most of them are made).

WHAT PEOPLE LOVE ABOUT

Champagne

- Its fine bubbles and snowy crown.
- Its vivacity, energy, depth, poise, class and chic.
- Its range of allusions and flavours (lemon, cream, hazels, apples, plum, bread, brioche, toast, biscuit).
- Its symbolic power: the great signifier of celebration, and a universal metaphor for high living and luxury.

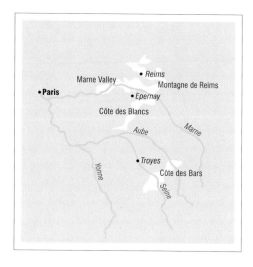

No French wine region lies further north than Champagne. Its wines, freshly fermented, are undrinkable: wincingly sour and sharp, like lemon juice. If they were bottled in that form, they would struggle to find customers. Instead, three years and a transformation later, they achieve the highest prices in the wine world. How does this nest of caterpillars metamorphose into a skyful of butterflies?

The answer is the secondary fermentation process described on page 70. That process is what puts the bubbles into the wine – but, just as importantly, it adds a yeasty fullness and creaminess to the aroma and flavour profile. Usually, too, a little sugar is added at the very end of the process to counter Champagne's spike of acidity. Once those enriching elements are there, the acidity itself is suddenly welcome, vivacious, enchanting, refreshing. In the wine world, everything really is a question of balance.

Geographically, the Champagne region is a braid of low, chalky hills rippling through the middle of the Seine river basin. This far north, not every slope catches enough sun to get the grapes ripe. Much of Champagne's land is good only for sugar beet. The most favoured villages call their vineyards Grand Cru; the second tier, Premier Cru. Blanc de Blancs means a Champagne made from Chardonnay alone, while Blanc de Noirs can be made from either of the region's black grapes: Pinot Noir and Pinot Meunier. Brut signifies a roundedly dry Champagne and Extra Brut very dry. Sec, Demi-Sec and Doux are progressively sweeter.

As far as complications go, that's it. Champagne is France's simplest wine region to understand. Most of its wines, indeed, don't even have a vintage date: they are made by blending together different vintages to create something with a consistent style, year in and year out. (If you do see a vintage date on the bottle, it should mark a generous summer.) Champagne prides itself on only selling its wines when its creators consider them ready to drink – but the best Champagnes, as lean and as fit as East African athletes, can run for decades or longer. The fizz gradually disappears, but the subtleties of aroma and flavour multiply harmonically.

OPPOSITE This giant chalk pit, hidden underneath the streets of Reims, was dug by Roman slaves ordered to cut building stone. Their ghosts enjoy a happier afterlife, nourished on Taittinger Champagne.

The Loire Valley

TRY A Sauvignon-based white from Sancerre, Pouilly-Fumé, Menetou-Salon or Quincy and compare it with one from New Zealand's Marlborough region: the Loire version will be less overtly grassy and fruity than its southern-hemisphere rival, but should be stonier and more vinous.

TRY A dry (Sec) Chenin-based white from Vouvray or Saumur and compare it with a South African Chenin Blanc: note the difference which South Africa's warmth makes in changing the character of the grape.

TRY A Chinon or Saumur-Champigny with a Médoc or Haut-Médoc red: the wines have a similar profile, but the Loire Valley's climate will almost always give greater vivacity and edge.

WHAT PEOPLE LOVE ABOUT

Loire Valley Wines

+ The zippy, stony, food-friendly freshness of the dry whites.
+ The vivid poise, aromatic intricacies, complexity of flavour and ability to age for decades of the best sweet whites.
+ Their easy-going, richly brocaded rosé wines.
+ The almost shocking impact of the dark, crunchy Cabernet-based reds.

France's longest river idles north from the country's volcanic heart. By Orléans, it has turned west. It then lollops gently west through a lush garden landscape before reaching the sea amid the ropes and cranes of St Nazaire. Its 1,020 km (634 miles) take it past many vineyards along the way. Do they have anything in common?

Yes: freshness. A little bracingly lean Gamay marks the source. Sauvignon Blanc then dominates in the eastern Loire; Chenin Blanc takes over the relay in the centre; and Melon de Bourgogne (the Muscadet grape) finishes the river's story in the west. Each of these varieties is characterized by vivid acidity and a crisp, mouthwatering profile; if you have a plate of oysters in front of you, then no region can provide a better range of wine partners than the Loire Valley. Sauvignon in Sancerre and Pouilly-Fumé smells less grassy and more stony than in New Zealand; Muscadet (especially when bottled *sur lie*, or directly off its yeast lees)

tastes of taut lemons with a little bready richness. And Chenin Blanc?

That depends. It depends in part since Chenin has so many incarnations: dry (Sec), medium-dry (Demi-Sec) and sweet (often called Moelleux here). That freshness never leaves it, but it is capable of taking on a huge number of inflections, from stone and apple in dry wines like Jasnières and Vouvray Sec to something much chewier and more substantial in Savennières and sometimes in Saumur and Anjou. The great sweet wines of the region (names to look out for include Vouvray, Coteaux de l'Aubance, Coteaux du Layon and Bonnezeaux) squelch with orchard fruits, and ooze honey, wax and marzipan.

The Loire's soft, plush pink wines are perennially popular, and there are red wines, too – especially on the warmest limestone vineyards between Tours and Angers. Saumur-Champigny, Bourgueil and Chinon are three of the names to note. Here, Cabernet Franc takes the lead in creating curranty reds which can almost take freshness to extremes. A cool year leaves a grassy print. Hot summers, by contrast, create dark, glinting, perfumed wines taut with energy, the fruit dashed across them in painterly fury.

OPPOSITE Castles conjured from fairy tales attest to the Loire's past wealth. Château du Nozet (which once belonged to Louis XV's illegitimate daughter) is maintained today by Baron de Ladoucette's fine Pouilly-Fumé.

Alsace

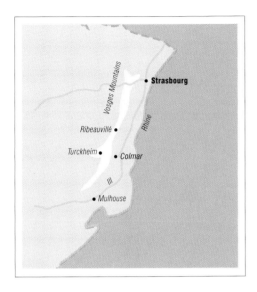

Alsace is where France faces Germany. Affably: Strasbourg belies its position as France's most easterly city, and one lying well to the north of Dijon, with a congenial climate. Colmar itself, among the vines, is a drier city than Bordeaux (502 mm is the 40-year average, compared with Bordeaux's 833 mm). Why? Look up to the forest-cloaked Vosges mountains, which survey the vineyards. Their peaks empty the clouds which pile in from the west. We have crossed, in fact, into the upper Rhine Valley: Germany's Baden lies across the river.

So is this where you will find France's most Germanic white wines? Yes, in that most are white. Yes, in that you will almost always find grape varieties named on labels. Yes: just look at those tall green bottles. Yes, too, in that many of them nowadays carry sweetness on their lips.

No, though, in that many remain dry and almost all are strong, even heady, in a way

that few German wines are. No, in that acidity levels are rarely as high in Alsace as they are in Germany. And no, in that they have a structured, food-loving vinosity which is very French. Spice, too, lurks in the hills here to an extent matched by no German region, not even Rheinpfalz (see page 161).

Riesling, as in Germany, is the grandee: intricate, authoritative, the classical music of the vineyards. Nowadays, too, it provides the most reliably dry and naturally well-balanced wines of the region. Gewurztraminer is the amply proportioned, scent-bomb seductress. Muscat, pushing its northern limits here, is unexpectedly dry, sometimes constrained, even catty. Pinot Gris can be Alsace incarnate: doughy, rich, chewy, complex, oily. Pinot Blanc (and its secret partner, Auxerrois) offers fresh, simply fruity charm; Sylvaner is sappier and earthier. There is pale Pinot Noir if you feel like red. The better vineyards call themselves Grand Cru; deliberately sweet wines are labelled Vendange Tardive (late harvest) or Séléction des Grains Nobles (a selection of botrytis-affected berries). Deliberately? Many wines in Alsace are, so to speak, accidentally sweet, thanks to lower yields and later harvesting than in the past, with no clue as to their sweetness on the label. Prepare, as you pull the cork, for anything.

OPPOSITE A summer night draws on in Riquewihr – which means that lots of pork and scented, rich white wine is beckoning. Perfect after a long day hiking in the Vosges.

TRY A dry Alsace Riesling and compare it with a dry-style German Riesling (look for the words Trocken or Halbtrocken) as well as a Riesling from Australia's Clare Valley. You will find major differences, proving just how expressive this grape variety is.

TRY An Alsace Pinot Gris alongside an Italian Pinot Grigio. In most cases, the Alsace wine will be more characterful and less dry than the Italian one: a function of greater ripeness and lower yields.

TRY An Alsace Gewurztraminer, and match it against an Argentinian Torrontés and a Viognier from the Rhône Valley (if possible, the expensive Condrieu). Compare the perfumes – and note the different styles of weight, texture and aroma when you sip.

WHAT PEOPLE LOVE ABOUT

Alsace Wines

+ The scent and spice of many of the whites.
+ The intrinsic richness, headiness and low acid levels of many of the whites.
+ The food-friendliness of the genuinely dry wines.
+ The voluptuous, almost decadent quality of the sweeter wines.
+ The wide range of soil types in the region, providing dappled wine flavours.

The Rhône Valley

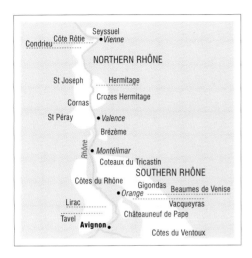

The Rhône is a river in a hurry. From its Swiss glacier origins at 1,753 metres to its final dissolution in the Camargue delta, it bustles south, cutting France's narrowest major river corridor as it does so. There are Swiss wines made on the banks of the Rhône, but most of those we associate with this river are French. They form two groups.

The vineyards of the northern Rhône, between Vienne and Valance, are opportunist. A foothold, a niche, a terrace: wherever the sun lingers, on the steep slopes of granite, schist and mica, the vines hang on with the tenacity of freestyle climbers. Syrah, here, is teased towards a racy, pure-fruited and sometimes smoky ripeness in red wines such as Hermitage, Crozes-Hermitage and St Joseph; Viognier, by contrast, grows rich and succulent in white Condrieu, and the two are often mingled (a little Viognier to a lot of Syrah) in red Côte Rôtie. Cornas, in a warm limestone amphitheatre, provides the biggest and

chewiest reds of the northern Rhône, though even these are lean by any universal red-wine gauge. Marsanne and Roussanne are the two white grapes that combine to statuesque effect for white Hermitage, Crozes-Hermitage, St Joseph and St Péray. Then the vineyards take a break.

They reappear as the river relaxes among the vast boulderfields of the south. This is a different place: sun, lavender, olive trees, jasmine. French accents now twang; fabrics are busily patterned; we have reached the land where Van Gogh saw the sky explode. It's expansive, too: 24 times more wine is produced in the southern Rhône than the north. Its leading appellation, Châteauneuf du Pape, sets the tone: this is the gentle giant among French reds, a rich and alcoholic blend of Grenache with other red grapes, usually including Syrah and Mourvèdre. Other reds are lighter (like many of those from the Côtes du Rhône) and sometimes brisker (when, for example, grown on the north-facing slopes of Gigondas), but there is always a southern ease, an mellow affability, about them. There are more white wines, too: at best fragrant with summer blossoms and rich, full and mouthfilling.

What do the two have in common? The headstrong river aside, very little.

OPPOSITE The hill of Hermitage commands the river – and its smoky, darting, incisive red wines and viscous, low-acid, scent-saturated whites take its mineral authority around the tables of the world.

TRY A red Crozes-Hermitage and compare it with a Barossa Shiraz from Australia to see how wide the Syrah's stylistic range can be.

TRY Compare a Côte Rôtie or a Hermitage with a Châteauneuf du Pape to illustrate the huge difference in growing conditions (soil and climate) between the northern and southern Rhône.

TRY Experiment with white wines from the Rhône Valley, from the simplest (white Côtes du Rhône) to the grandest (Hermitage Blanc). They make an intriguing alternative to Chardonnay and white Burgundy.

TRY If you want to understand what the increasingly fashionable Viognier grape is capable of, try Condrieu.

WHAT PEOPLE LOVE ABOUT

Rhône Valley Wines

- The fragrance, finesse and purity of northern Rhône reds.
- The softness, meatiness and breadth of southern Rhône reds.
- The weighty, textured richness and blossomy perfumes of Rhône whites.
- A savoury quality and a rugged, unpolished honesty about many traditional Rhône wines, especially reds.
- Fine value for money among the best Côtes du Rhône and Côtes du Rhône-Villages wines (including Beaumes de Venise, Cairanne and Vacqueyras), and Costières de Nîmes, too.

The South of France

TRY Compare Bandol, Cahors and Madiran: three of the biggest, gutsiest, most challenging and most rewarding reds France has to offer. Decant them well in advance of serving.

TRY A St Chinian, a Pic St Loup and a Corbières. Look for depth and richness in St Chinian, freshness and perfume in Pic St Loup, and rugged wildness in Corbières.

TRY Experiment with some of the more expensive wines from Roussillon (they may also be labelled Vins de Pays des Côtes Catalanes) and compare them with wines from Priorat in Spain, where varieties and growing conditions are not dissimilar.

TRY Contrast a good Bergerac with a good Côtes de Castillon from Bordeaux. Can you tell the difference? The two appellations lie next door to one another.

TRY Compare a top Cahors with an ambitious Argentinian Malbec. The Argentinian wine may be bigger and more exuberant, but the Cahors will probably be tighter, tauter, more tannic and more food-friendly.

OPPOSITE The ruined Cathar fortress of Château d'Aiguilar surveys the vineyards of Fitou and Corbières – and hills prickly with scented *garrigue*, too.

Provence, Corsica, Languedoc, Roussillon, the Pyrenees: from the Alps to the Atlantic, there are few spots in France's far south where the vine truly struggles to ripen. A sea of vines, then, greenly echoing the bright blue of the Mediterranean? Not exactly. Even under a generous sun, the fundamental inequalities of soil and climate apply. The best wines of the south form an archipelago of scattered islands.

Provence … you'll be thinking of pale, dry silver-pink rosé wines: a leitmotiv of countless seaside holidays, terrace lunches and afternoon siestas. The best are an essay in delicacy and restraint. There is more, though, most notably the grand red Bandol, where Mourvèdre achieves rugged beauty and great textural depths in a hot limestone amphitheatre behind the naval town of Toulon. Bandol aside, you may find Provence's whites more impressive than its reds: the hills climb steeply from the sea, and growing conditions are often cooler and fresher than raw latitude suggests. The same is true for mountainous Corsica. Fine wine will one day be decoded in the white limestone rubble beneath La Baux, in the slopes which prefigure Mont Sainte-Victoire and in the fretful relief of Corsica's twisting hillsides; for now, though, all is research.

Languedoc has two faces: the plain and the hills. Vins de Pays dominate the plain: easy-going varietal wines whose point of difference with global competitors is often a little ingrained French delicacy. Those made from local grape varieties tend to outclass the international standards, a few celebrated exceptions aside. It's up on the hills, though, that Languedoc is finally achieving the destiny it was cheated of during the twentieth century: the creation of wines (mostly red, but some whites too) which reflect the stony drama of the landscape and the untilled savagery of sun, thorn, herb and boulder. The appellation system is in mid-evolution at present, but names to watch out for include St Chinian, Faugères, Pic St Loup, La Clape, Minervois and Corbières. You might imagine sturdy weight and flesh would be the chief asset of these southerners, yet it's their movingly wild perfumes I treasure. The sparkling wines and oaked whites of cool Limoux form a surprising contrast.

Roussillon is France's portion of sunny Catalonia. The heat rises further; schist, slate and granite tussle with limestone; old-vine Grenache combines with Syrah and Mourvèdre to provide reds which can match Châteauneuf for weight and sweetness, though they replace its soft, meaty warmth with a firmer mineral grip. Few doubt that Roussillon will produce great wine one day. Look out, too, for the sometimes majestic fortified wines of Banyuls, Maury and Rivesaltes.

And South-West France? Crowded together under this vague name is a characterful band of brigands. Most urbane of these are the cluster of appellations around the town of Bergerac (and including

WHAT PEOPLE LOVE ABOUT

Southern French Wines

- The exuberance, wildness and warmth of the reds.
- The sometimes unexpected freshness and vivacity of the whites.
- The sense of exploration and discovery which this region offers.
- Its pretty, dry rosé wines, for summer lunches and outdoor eating.
- Its comforting fortified wines.

RIGHT Vineyards, pines and the scented scrub beyond: the easy relationship between viticulture and nature is summarized by these vineyards near Vidauban in the Côtes de Provence.

the luxuriously sweet Monbazillac): Bordeaux white varieties take on an extra creaminess here, and reds a savoury warmth. Cahors, surveying the serpentine River Lot, is where Malbec takes centre stage in France to dark, perfumed and occasionally shocking effect. The old Roman vineyards near Gaillac produce a little rainbow of characterful specialities, while Fronton returns a southern echo of Beaujolais, thanks to the peppery, gulpable charms of the Négrette grape. Côtes de Gascogne does much the same for white wine, thanks to local cunning with the workhorses Colombard and Ugni Blanc (Trebbiano).

Then comes one of France's least known grandees. Madiran, a vinous black hole at the centre of the Dax-Auch-Tarbes triangle, produces reds of unrivalled gravitational force. The Tannat grape, the clay soils and the sub-Pyrenean climate combine to produce wines whose tannic charge and depth of character can almost suck you over the event horizon. The reds of Côtes de St Mont are smaller, but cut from the same sturdy cloth. The whites of Jurançon, both dry and sweet, are bracing and invigorating, thanks to their mountain-fresh acidity (they grow in suntraps on the lower slopes of the Pyrenees) and the intrinsic qualities of the local grape Manseng, both Gros and Petit. Irouléguy, finally, provides a fresh-flavoured Basque finale to all this excitement.

FACT FILE: France

Fine wines The unrivalled world leader. Champagne, Burgundy and Bordeaux are the historical classics, respectively the world's greatest sparkling wines, light reds and medium-bodied reds. The best wines of the Rhône, Alsace and the Loire are unquestionably fine, too, and I would add the muscular trio of Bandol, Cahors and Madiran to that list.

Fun wines Hundreds. My list of favourites includes growers' Champagnes, Demi-Sec wines from the Loire, Beaujolais, and a sprinkling of specialities from the south of France, like Bergerac, Marcillac, La Clape, Pic St Loup and St Chinian.

National strengths Huge diversity and variety; almost uniform food-friendliness; an intrinsic sense of balance and delicacy; the willingness to allow the natural qualities of grape variety and vineyard to emerge in a wine, even if these may seem singular, strange or odd in the international context.

National weaknesses A torrent of names and complications for wine drinkers to try to understand; poor-quality labelling, with a frequent absence of background information and explanations; highly variable quality in some regions; some overpricing among France's acknowledged fine wines.

**PROJECT 11
PLACES: Italy**

Few painted Renaissance landscapes are complete without a vineyard; few Italian country-dwellers have never made wine. Wine is as intimate a part of Italian life as pasta or coffee. This closeness means that Italy's garden of grape varieties and library of wines has lasted, almost unscathed, until the twenty-first century. Even the most scholarly wine enthusiast expects constant surprises from charming, chaotic Italy.

Northern Italy

Does Italy have a Burgundy? If so, it is Piedmont. This is the land of the small grower rather than the large estate. Hills plunge, swirl and spin: the logic of the single vineyard is paramount. And the great grape variety of Piedmont, Nebbiolo, is very nearly as difficult to tease to perfection as is Pinot Noir. It needs long, stubborn ripening, well into the heart of autumn, by which time the fog (*la nebbia*) has come to clothe everything with mystery and mistrust, and nimble white dogs are sniffing out hidden truffles in the silence of the night.

Barolo and Barbaresco – craggy, tannic, acidic, but at best perfumed and enticing, too – succeed as irregularly as does red burgundy. This being Italy, though, there is a host of alternatives: plummy red Dolcetto; energetic though sometimes biting red Barbera; the orchard-fruited white Arneis; and frothy, frivolous white Moscato. Don't forget delicate dry white Gavi, either, from hillsides just north of basil-perfumed Genoa.

Does Italy have a Bordeaux? If so, it is Tuscany. Here the estates are bigger, more aristocratic, lavished with *castelli* (castles, châteaux). The Sangiovese grape has an easy assurance to it altogether beyond touchy Nebbiolo. Great Tuscan wines breathe refinement (as do their claretty counterparts). Chianti is like a walk in an olive grove at dusk: it's a wine of pale light and dark shadows. There should be a sour quality to its acidity, and a briskness to its tannins. The limey local soils – *galestro* – leave a stony trace. It's laurel and coffee; it's complicated plot-lines; it's a whisper in a courtyard. Brunello di Montalcino is more masterful and muscular than Chianti; Vino Nobile di Montepulciano is a little riper and rounder; and coastal Bolgheri (a great location for Cabernet and Merlot as well as Sangiovese) more international – though indubitably fine. Morellino di Scansano brings a seaside suppleness to Sangiovese.

There is much more, though, to northern Italy than these big guns. The Adige Valley, up which tomato-laden lorries thunder their way past Trento and Bolzano towards Innsbruck and Munich, is the source of many of Italy's mountain wines: fresh whites, often from international varieties like Chardonnay and Sauvignon, as well as rose-reds from Schiava, the 'slave girl', and deeper though always brisk reds based on Teroldego Rotaliano and Lagrein.

To the east of Lake Garda, on a series of once-volcanic hills, vines grow with the

TRY Compare a Barolo or Barbaresco with a Taurasi, to contrast two great Italian red grape varieties (Nebbiolo and Aglianico) and two very different climates.

TRY A good (single-vineyard) Soave and a good Fiano di Avellino to prove that Italy's reputation for trivial white wines is not merited.

TRY To see how well international varieties can fare in Italy, try Merlot- and Cabernet-based wines from Bolgheri, Chardonnay from elsewhere in Tuscany, Sauvignon Blanc from Alto Adige and Friuli, and Syrah from Sicily.

TRY Compare a Primitivo from Puglia with a Zinfandel from California: despite the heat of Puglia, the latter is likely to be still sweeter and richer.

TRY Modern Chianti Classico, strangely enough, is allowed to contain up to 20% Cabernet or Merlot. Try one made from such a blend, and compare it with a pure-Sangiovese Chianti Classico (the back labels should help you make the varietal diagnosis).

OPPOSITE Soave and Chianti are typically Italian in that they exist in cheap, sometimes rough versions which share little with the best. 'Classico' is a clue, but the producer's name is safest.

vegetative fury of jungle creepers. Pretty little lightweight Bardolino hugs the lakeside, but it is Valpolicella and Soave which play Romeo and Juliet, here in Verona's backyard. The fragrant cherrystone fruit of the former deepens into sweetness with Recioto and dry strength with Amarone. Much Soave is a flighty white – but the best is almost chewy, and full of marzipan depths. Lugana, from the southern end of the same lake, is based on a local cousin of the fish-loving Verdicchio grape.

Fizzy Prosecco heightens Venice's dreamy trance – but head towards Slovenia and you'll find some of Italy's most serious and gastronomically accomplished whites in Collio and Friuli. The best of the reds there are crunchy and currant-fresh.

'Bologna the fat', wallowing amid the River Po's flatlands, is less propitious for fine wines than it is for cheese, ham and sausage, but Lambrusco (the original is red, dry and challenging) and Sangiovese di Romagna wash the fine food down. On the Adriatic coast, meanwhile, the white Verdicchio provides one of Italy's greatest fish partners – to the extent that the sturdy Rosso Conero is often unjustly overlooked. Umbria, Italy's landlocked green heart, is best known for the affable white Orvieto, but the almost shockingly tannic red Montefalco Sagrantino and the rather more urbane red Torgiano offer profounder satisfactions.

RIGHT A chaos of hills, punctuated by woods, villas, and silent, private cypresses: we're in the heart of Chianti. It's always faintly mysterious, despite the bright sunshine.

Southern Italy

WHAT PEOPLE LOVE ABOUT

Italian Wines

- The poise, energy, thrust and depth of character of the reds.
- The delicacy, grace and food-friendliness of the whites.
- The endless variety, interest and intrigue of the lesser-known grape varieties and wines.
- The easy, effortless role of wine in daily life and eating in Italy.

OPPOSITE Fans of Lampedusa's *The Leopard* will relish this Sicilian vineyard nameboard at the Contessa Entellina estate of Donnafugata, well above the seaside swelter. Corleone is not far away, either.

Rome's wine, in principle, is no more ambitious than Venice's Prosecco. Almondy Frascati is the best known: a white of such quenching simplicity that it might have trickled directly from a hillside spring. Marino is an alternative. (I'm not being dismissive: sometimes simplicity is perfection.)

To find a deep red, you need to cross the Apennines to Abruzzo, where Montepulciano (grape variety not place) helps make reds with true southern stuffing and texture. Indeed the rest of Italy's Adriatic coast, all the way down to its Puglian heel, is red-wine country, and rewarding for bargain-hunters, too: there's more Montepulciano in Molise, then inland you'll find the rich, assertive and age-worthy Aglianico del Vulture. The dormant volcano of Monte Vulture is where southern Italy's greatest red grape variety meets the soils it craves. Puglia's Salento peninsula sees Negroamaro and Primitivo (Zinfandel) flourish in crimson-soiled flatland vineyards cooled by a breeze from two seas,

giving red wines with an intrinsic sweetness and fleshiness that you'll rarely find further north. Squinzano, Copertino and Salice Salentino are all names to jot. The local tradition of allowing these reds a few barrel years to relax and soften gives convincingly delicious results, too.

Rome … and Naples? In the classical era, it was just to the north of Naples that Italy's greatest wine came into being: Falernian sold at four times the price of ordinary wine in the bars of Pompeii. Naples, indeed, can still claim to have great wine on its doorstep: the rich red Taurasi (based on late-ripening Aglianico grapes) is southern Italy's finest, and the contrasting whites Greco di Tufo (full, chewy and stony) and Fiano di Avellino (light, fresh and floral) can both be outstanding, too, even if the grandeur of Falernian itself is now lost in history. The poverty and lack of development of Basilicata and Calabria may have held its wines in check, but there is no shortage of intriguing grape varieties here, and they will prove the region's ace in the years ahead.

As Sicily has proved. Traditionally, this was the home of Marsala, a fortified wine of British invention once destined for naval thirsts but nowadays usually sloshed into zabaglione. The best (like olive oil, revered as Virgine) is dry yet smooth, burnished and buttery. It is Sicily's ambitious table wines, though – based both on international varieties and native grape varieties like the red Nero d'Avola and Nerello Mascalese and the white Catarratto, Inzolia and Grillo –

which have won the island's try-harder producers a reputation for both value and innovation in recent years. (Many, alas, fail to try at all: Sicilian overproduction has been a long-running European scandal.) Don't be misled by geographical location: by planting vines in the high hills of central Sicily, it is possible to make wines far livelier, fresher and more scented than a latitude lower than that of Athens would suggest. Sicilian labels, too, are surprisingly fresh and accessible. Most of the island's star wines in recent years have been varietals produced under no more specific a description than the IGT of 'Sicilia'.

What of southern Italy's other great island? Sardinia's Aragonese history has left it with a legacy of Spanish grape varieties: for Cannonau, read Garnacha (or Grenache); for Carignano, read Cariñena (or Carignan). Both flourish here, the former sweetly and the latter more drily and dustily, alongside native red varieties Monica and Girò, and the white Nuragus. Red Bovale (both Sardo and Grande) may be related to Spain's Bobal. Fennel-scented Vermentino, a favourite along the Mediterranean seaboard (it's called Rolle in France), provides many of the island's whites.

Italy's footnote, and Europe's last southern landfall, is the island of Pantelleria, just 50 miles off the Tunisian coast. Muscat, unforgettably called Zibbibo here, is sun-dried to an orange-liqueur richness.

RIGHT Not an inch of soil is wasted along the coast between Capri and Salerno. Vineyards tussle with citrus groves to make the tourist-friendly red and white Costa d'Amalfi wines.

FACT FILE: Italy

Fine wines Italy's finest wines are mostly red. They include Barolo, Barbaresco, Chianti Classico and Chianti Rufina, Brunello di Montalcino, Amarone and Taurasi, as well as a wide variety of highly ambitious reds made under the flexible IGT (Indicazione Geografica Tipica) rules in Bolgheri and elsewhere.

Fun wines Almost everything else. Note that fun, for Italians, doesn't preclude bitter flavours and high levels of acidity – as you may find with Barbera in Piedmont. It all makes sense with pasta! Most Italian whites are fun (and foamy-sweet Moscato is fun personified), but the best whites are beginning to achieve real grandeur, too.

National strengths Originality, diversity and character, as well as the sense that wine's mealtime context is never far away; few Italians wines fail at table.

National weaknesses Chaotic nomenclature; a disappointing recent readiness to allow international varieties into classical wine blends; wildly varying quality standards, even for wines which have won top DOCG (Denominazione di Origine Controllata et Garantita) status.

PROJECT 12
PLACES: Spain

Up in the lonely, high, treeless places, sprawling like penitents in a chaotic landscape, Spain's tough vines suck a living from the stony earth. Twenty years ago, many Spanish wines were tethered, like donkeys under a midday sun, to a set of sterile traditions. The last two decades have brought liberation. Spain is now inventive, proud, assured – and Spanish wine some of Europe's most exciting.

Spanish Wines

Let's begin this story of novelty with a glance back to tradition. Rioja is the Spanish red wine every drinker knows. More than most, a formula lies behind it: Tempranillo grown in clay and limestone in the upper Ebro Valley just south of Basque country, then blended and cosseted into mellowness in the sweet arms of an American white oak barrel. The vanilla-scented, easy-drinking wine which results is justly popular, and still provides the core of the region's appeal. Rioja has a leading edge, though. Growers (rather than large companies) working with individual vineyards, French oak and shorter ageing regimes are now producing much deeper, darker and more intensely flavoured wines. The result is that Rioja, like Bordeaux, is stylistically a more diverse place than it used to be.

Rioja, though, is not without its challengers. The most assured of these is Ribera del Duero, lining the banks of the river which, once it has crossed the Portuguese border, will carve its way through the rocky canyons of the port region. Ribera del Duero is higher than Rioja, with cooler nights; Tempranillo (here called Tinto Fino) produces wines of greater drama, depth and challenge, spelling out newness as emphatically as Gehry's metallic swirl for the Bilbao Guggenheim. Toro, to the west of Ribera del Duero, piles on the beefy flesh – and yes, the Tinta de Toro here is yet another name for Tempranillo. Between the two lies Rueda, where some of Spain's greenest, sheerest whites begin life. Verdejo is its key

grape, though Sauvignon Blanc can also play. (Cabernet Sauvignon, Merlot and Syrah, by the way, are likely to show up almost anywhere in Spain. A modernist outlook? Not really. It was simply that its traditions had undergone less refinement than in France or Italy as the late twentieth century's wine renaissance unfolded.)

An altogether different challenge to Rioja's supremacy is posed by Catalonia's great rockyard, Priorat. It is Garnacha and Cariñena rather than Tempranillo which take the lead here, digging their roots into a glittering slate locally called *llicorella*. The result is something more mineral than either Rioja or Ribera del Duero. Fruit flavours, in Priorat, acquire an almost medicinal density. Few wines leave their drinkers with a sense of shock and awe, but this is one of them. Montsant, girdling Priorat, provides an echo.

Other parts of busy Catalonia love to challenge Rioja's hegemony, too: Penedès, Conca de Barberá, Costers del Segre and Catalunya are all names you may see on bottles of ambitious red. These tend to be more international in style, though Spain's warmth courses through them like blood. Catalonia is also the home of Spain's great sparkling wine, Cava. 'Great' in this context refers as much to volume as quality. The grapes, in fact, can come from elsewhere in Spain, though the vast majority are sourced locally; Chardonnay and Pinot Noir play a role in the best wines, but local varieties Macabeo, Xarel-lo and Parellada leave their flowery, appley stamp more consistently.

TRY Compare a Rioja, a Ribera del Duero and a Toro to see how climate, soil and altitude can modify the character of Tempranillo (though check the back label for details of whether the wine is aged in French or American oak, too).

TRY Compare a Priorat with ambitious reds from France's Roussillon and Portugal's Douro Valley: these are all savage, hot and rocky regions whose wines tend to have pronounced mineral characters.

TRY For outstanding value for money from Spain, look out for Jumilla, Calatayud, Cariñena and Montsant. No sparkling wine offers better value than Cava, too.

OPPOSITE Vega Sicilia was the nineteenth-century Ribera del Duero pioneer, seasoning Spain's Tempranillo with Bordeaux varieties. Late harvesting and lavish oak cossetting add to the rich, low-yield grandeur.

Spanish Wines
+ The softness, sweetness
  and mellowness of Spain's
  traditional red wines, especially
  those from Rioja.
+ The power and excitement of
  its new-generation red wines.
+ The value for money of less
  well-known, up-and-coming
  Spanish wines.
+ Spain's easy incorporation of
  international grape varieties
  into its fast-developing
  domestic scene.

OPPOSITE The church and the
vineyard have a close relationship
– sometimes even physically, as
here near Haro in Rioja Alta.

Bearing in mind the high production costs of sparkling wine made by the same methods as in Champagne, Cava remains astonishingly good value for money.

There is one part of Spain where climate and soil conspire to create something very far from the bright, shimmering aridity of vineyard, mirage and windmill. Galicia, Spain's stubby finger pointing west into the Atlantic, is a cool, green, wet land of slender, fragrant white wines grown on granite wherever a steep hill smiles southwards. Albariño, here as in Portugal's vinho verde country to the south, pitches to be Iberia's Riesling. Godello can be as complex, but is fuller in flavour. Perhaps surprisingly, reds (based on the Mencía grape, capable both of a light-hearted fruitiness as well as something denser and more mineral) work well in Valdeorras, Ribeira Sacra and, especially, the slate-terraced Bierzo.

The rest of the country is a quilt of different DO (Denominación de Origen) areas, each with something to prove – and each busy trying to prove it. Here are a few of the best. Spain is in such a ferment at present, though, that it would be foolish to leave any cork unpulled.

Rioja's neighbour Navarra has an assured way with red, white and sweet wines; substantial plantings of Cabernet Sauvignon and Chardonnay are part of the reason, but the cool of the north is another. Somontano, loitering airily under the Pyrenees, even dares to plant Pinot Noir and Gewurztraminer. The try-harder trio of Campo de Borja, Cariñena and Calatayud seem close to Navarra or Somontano on the map, but the warmth of the Ebro Valley and its tumble towards the Mediterranean mean

that these sites are better suited to sturdy Grenache and Tempranillo.

Spain's heart (La Mancha: Quixote country) is also Europe's largest single sprawl of vines – and sprawl is very much the word for the low, straggling, widely spaced plants which patch out a life here. Most are the undistinguished white Airén, their grapes beckoned by the brandy still, but Tempranillo (this grape of many aliases calls itself Cencibel here) dominates in the enclave of Valdepeñas. Valencia and Murcia, basking in Mediterranean sunlight, foster another batch of self-improving DOs. Jumilla is my favourite, perhaps because I have a soft spot for its gruff red grape Monastrell (known as Mourvèdre in France and Mataro in Australia and California). Manchuela and Utiel-Requena are both high, and both put red Bobal to good use. In Spain's far west, hard against the Portuguese border, the new region of Ribera del Guadiana promises much, too.

Spain's far south is dominated by the sherry region, of which more over the page. There are other, tangily strong wines here, too: sherry-like styles from Condado da Huelva and (unfortified) from Montilla-Moriles, and sweeter, richer wines from the Málaga DO. Even here, though, innovation is trotting the hills: look out for unfortified dry wines from a huge range of international varieties in the Sierras de Málaga, and for Vinos de la Tierra (Spain's equivalent of France's Vins de Pays) from the highlands around Granada. Spain's islands, finally, have been garlanded with DOs of their own (two on Mallorca and an astonishing eleven in the Canaries); quality, though, limps some way behind the mainland pace.

Sherry

TRY Drinking Fino or Manzanilla sherry chilled, in normal wine glasses, with a wide range of fish and seafood dishes. The combinations will be better than you ever imagined – provided that the bottle (or half bottle) is freshly opened.

TRY The oldest dry and sweet Oloroso blends you can find: these are the treasure-chest wines kept hidden at the back of every bodega, and often bear resonant names (like Gonzalez Byass's sweet Matúsalem or Valdespino's dry Don Gonzalo). Versions called VOS are at least 20 years old, and VORS at least 30 years old. You may also see other indications of age (12, 15, 20 or 30 years old) on the label.

WHAT PEOPLE LOVE ABOUT

Sherry

+ The fresh, lively, bread-like appeal, mouthwatering with umami, of great Fino and Manzanilla sherry.
+ The aromatic refinement of great Amontillado and Palo Cortado.
+ The depth and profundity of great Oloroso sherries, both dry and sweet.

OPPOSITE Landscape, dreamscape, moonscape? At times, the vast, blanched vineyards of Jerez can seem like all three. Strange things happen to the wines, too, in this unique location.

Sherry is a world of its own. In North African latitudes, sunk amongst the lowest lands of a high country, the sherry region lounges in the sunshine like a giant pearl. Palm trees break the blue of the sky; green vines sip moisture from the tiny pores in its dazzlingly chalky soils. Those vines are the Palomino variety (also known as Listán). They make a dull wine with little personality. Do one of two crazy things to those wines, though, and they change. Their personality blossoms.

Crazy things? Well, no one sane would let mould grow on their new wine. And no one sane would allow the warm, open air to bite so deeply into it that it turned walnut brown. These two acts, though, produce wines of strange, compelling beauty.

Let's begin with the mould. In Spanish, it is called *flor*, or 'flower'. It's a carpet of yeast which grows thickly on new, pale, lightly fortified dry Palomino wine. Why? No one knows. Perhaps because the hot, high heart of Spain sucks moisture in from the sea. After a few years' ageing, the resulting wine is pale, bready, yeasty, pungent with acetaldehyde – and mouthwateringly delicious. If it comes from the sherry towns of Jerez or Puerto de Santa Maria, it is called Fino; if it comes from the seaside town of Sanlúcar de Barrameda, where the *flor* grows most thickly of all, it is called Manzanilla.

And the other crazy act? Darker sherries, like Olorosos, are fortified more heavily than lighter ones (to 18% abv rather than 15%); the *flor* cannot grow on wines of this strength. Instead, they are massaged by

penetrating fingers of warm Andalucian air. This oxidation would ruin white burgundy, but it's the making of dark sherry. It leaves the wines with unrivalled bite and tang.

Consistency comes via the cunning 'solera system' used in the sherry region, which blends and ages simultaneously: tier upon tier of casks are partially emptied and partially filled, ad infinitum. The process mingles their contents as successfully as human reproduction swirls genes.

All sherry begins dry. Sweeter sherries are created by adding sweeter wines based on dark Pedro Ximénez or light Moscatel grapes. Amontillado is, for purists, an elderly Fino (in Sanlúcar called Pasada), which has shed its *flor* and begun ageing oxidatively; most are blended, semi-sweet and semi-dark. Palo Cortado is a sherry that began life as a Fino, then abandoned its *flor* prematurely.

FACT FILE: Spain

Fine wines A fast-changing scene. Venerable, lengthily aged Rioja (and Vega Sicilia's celebrated Unico) have been polished to a sheen by time before bottling; but Spain's modern classics (such as single-site Rioja, the elite of Ribera del Duero and the tortured masterpieces of Priorat) are bottled younger, and crave collectors' cellars to reach maturity. Toro, Navarra and Penedès are snapping at their heels. The finest sherries (especially traditional blends incorporating wines of great age) are as great, though far cheaper.

Fun wines 'Fun' in Spain rarely means frivolous or juicy – but if you have a taste for reds on the Mount Rushmore scale, Spain has a huge amount to offer, from a dozen or more DOs (such as Jumilla, Calatayud and Cariñena). Paradoxically, there is lots of fun in Spain for those who crave the opposite: very light reds tamed into meekness by a long stint in (usually American) oak. Look for these among less expensive Riojas and the wines of Valdepeñas. Spain is short of good dry whites, but there is a third sort of fun in the inexpensive sweet fortified whites, often based on Moscatel grapes, from Valencia and elsewhere.

National strengths Power, warmth, value and innovation.

National weaknesses Many wines are still coarsely made, and keeping abreast of Spain's rapidly unfolding wine scene requires study. The readiness to use international varieties before native ones is welcomed by some, while others feel it obscures Spain's authenticity. Some Spanish wines (especially those in heavy bottles) are priced with mad ambition.

**PROJECT 13
PLACES:
North America**

Vines grow in all 50 American states as well as four Canadian provinces. They flourish best in the western coastal states, where a great sea mitigates the winter freeze, tames the vicious caprices of a continental spring and softens the rigours of a portcullis-like autumn. Wherever human ingenuity can coax *Vitis vinifera* into fruitfulness, though, there will be an American or Canadian ready to live the dream.

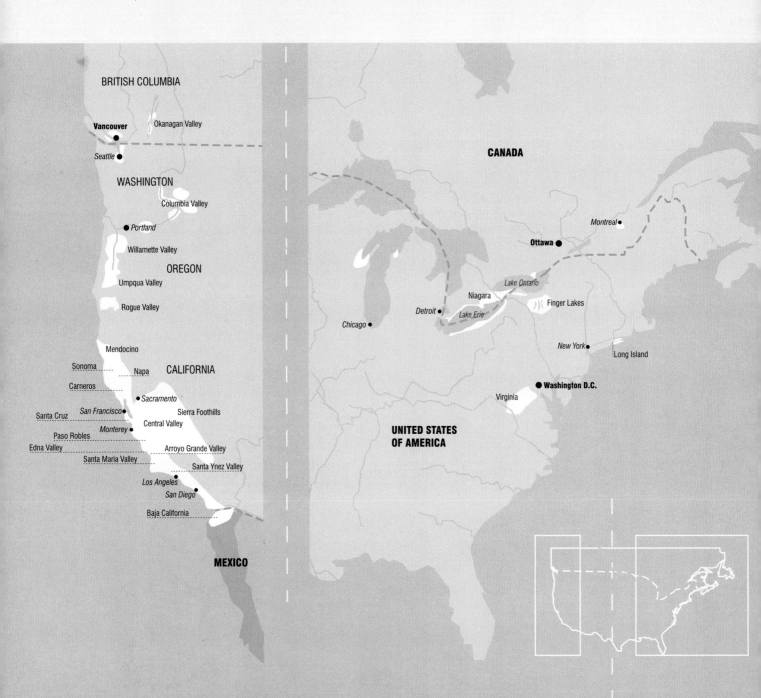

California

California dominates North American wine production: nine out of ten American bottles of wine begin life as grapes swelling in the state's golden light. Just how much of that light the bunches receive is not, as in Europe, a question of how far north or south they grow. Instead, listen for the roar of the ocean. The North Pacific Gyre sends cold waters plunging southwards from Canada's British Columbia to Mexico's Baja California; prevailing north-westerly winds, too, rotate cold sub-surface seawater towards the sky. California's penetrating fingers of fog, invading the land like a stealthy nocturnal tsunami, are the result.

Generally, then, the nearer a vineyard is to the coast in California, the foggier will be its mornings, and the cooler and fresher will be its wines. The Anderson Valley and Russian River Valley north of San Francisco are two examples, but you'll also find cool sites much further south – such as Edna Valley and Arroyo Grande near San Luis

Obispo, or the Santa Rita Hills in the Santa Ynez Valley near Los Angeles. Inland vineyards (in the Central Valley, for example, or the Sierra Foothills) are furnace-hot, and their wines can be some of the richest in the world. There's every nuance between – and most notably, in the central zones of the Napa Valley, the kind of long, generous summer warmth and extravagant light perfect for teasing Cabernet Sauvignon to broad-backed, muscular perfection. The well-drained soils – loams, gravels, dust, sometimes of volcanic origin – of Rutherford, Oakville and Stags Leap nurture complexity as well as power. The valleys of Sonoma, a masterclass in the complexities of soil and site, offer intricately woven fugal variations.

There's another important distinction to make, too. California is home to some of the world's finest and most solicitous winemakers, and the result is an ever-expanding range of wines of telling originality and truth to place. America's prosperity means that these wines are seldom cheap, but nowhere else outside Europe is the quest for distinguished sites being pursued with such zeal. The state, however, is also home to some of the dullest, blandest and most insidiously sugary wines on the planet. Don't judge California by its big brands.

Most California wines are sold by grape variety, and California has forged its own, distinctively generous style for all of the world's favourites. Rippling Cabernet has already been mentioned, but California has

TRY Chardonnay and Pinot Noir from northern Sonoma, and compare them with equivalents from Burgundy: notice the wealth of flavour and silkiness of texture of the Californian Chardonnay, and the purity and roundness of the Californian Pinot. The burgundies will be more slender, perhaps sharper, though they may have more vinosity and finesse.

TRY An old-vine Zinfandel from the Sierra Foothills: look for brambly sweetness lifted by heady alcohol levels.

TRY A Napa Valley Cabernet Sauvignon, and compare it with a wine from Bordeaux's Médoc zones: notice the opulence, density and richness of the Napa wine, making even the heftiest Pauillac or St Julien seem relatively graceful and refreshing.

TRY A Syrah from California's Central Coast, and compare it with an Australian Shiraz: check out the softer, more relaxed balance of the Californian wine, and its lighter and more perfumed fruit style.

TRY Many of California's most exciting and successful wines are now blends: compare two or three with varietal equivalents from the same locations. You may find the blends more complex.

OPPOSITE It's Pinot, but with a distinctive Californian generosity: ripe berries and round-contoured, soft-textured flavours. Burgundy couldn't do that, even if it wanted to. We're lucky to have both.

WHAT PEOPLE LOVE ABOUT

Californian Wines

* The breadth and wealth of flavour of the white wines.
* The density, power and assurance of the red wines.
* Their stylistic diversity.
* The readiness of the greatest growers to respect their soils and skies by not deforming the natural balance of their wines.

RIGHT The nourishing light is a constant – but Sonoma's softly braided soil contours never repeat themselves. The fog's moisture feeds distinctive swags of lace lichen hanging from the oaks.

been no less successful with Chardonnay. This can, on occasion, be a meal in itself: rich, lactic and lingeringly sweet. The best, though, combine a textural richness with ample flavoury nuance and poise: bigger in contour and outline than anything northern Europe can produce, but as complex, as layered and as satisfying. Sauvignon Blanc is less assured, and always closer in style to that grape's ripest Bordeaux persona than the stony austerities of the Loire Valley or the leafy, passion-fruit pungency of New Zealand; Viognier is a promising newcomer. Pinot Noir, thanks to those cool, coastal locations, is more than holding its own. Once again, the fundamental dimensions of Californian Pinot place it in a different class to the best of Burgundy, but its poise, perfume and finesse can be winningly true to the grape's ideal. Rhône and Italian grape varieties, many reason, may be better suited to Californian conditions than those of northern France, so Syrah, Mourvèdre and Sangiovese are all on the march; white Marsanne and Roussanne, too.

In Zinfandel, of course, California has a world original. Only Australia's richest Shiraz wines can approach California's old-vine Zinfandels for sheer extravagance. Ripeness is all. A high percentage of California's oldest vines are Zinfandel, just as many of Australia's 'grandfather' vinestocks are Shiraz. The concentration, intensity and sometimes daunting alcohol levels which these low-yielding, deep-rooted octogenarians are capable of finding, for example, in the decomposed granites and languid sunsets of the Sierra Foothills make them the drinker's equivalent of gold-hunter's dynamite.

Oregon, Washington State and the Rest of the USA

TRY Compare Pinot Noir from Oregon's Willamette Valley with a red village burgundy from the Côte de Nuits, and a Willamette Pinot Gris with an Alsace example. Are there similarities? What are the differences? You may find a greater edge to the burgundy, and more depth of fruit and sweetness in the Alsace Pinot Gris – but try both with food, too, to see how that changes things.

TRY Compare Merlot from Washington State with Merlot from California: look for depth, vivacity and definition in the former, but more texture and a softer style of fruit in the latter. Could either be confused with Pomerol? If not, why not?

TRY A Syrah from Washington, and compare it with a Syrah from Mendoza in Argentina: which is fresher, denser, more perfumed?

WHAT PEOPLE LOVE ABOUT

Oregon and Washington State Wines

- The subtlety and lack of showiness of Oregon's Pinot, Chardonnay and Pinot Gris.
- The drama and impact of Washington State's Merlot and Syrah.

OPPOSITE A greener summer scene, in New York's Finger Lakes, than any in California. The home of the hybrid is now welcoming classic varieties, too.

Oregon is, visually speaking, the most European of America's wine landscapes. It's a rumpled, hilly land of changeable skies and mixed agriculture, of autumn bonfires and hedgerow bounty. As the summer shadows lengthen, growers (the big companies avoid Oregon) scan the skies with nervousness, hoping the harvest rain will hold off. Just like in Burgundy. And, just like in Burgundy, their hopes are often dashed.

You can almost guess the rest, even if you've never yet tasted a glass of Oregon wine. Forget California's hunks; beside them, Oregon's best feel slim. They are fresh, fine-grained, subtle, thought-provoking. (The worst can be dull, hard, tart.) Pinot Noir is a continuing quest whose greatest triumphs have been slower in coming than the pioneers hoped; and Pinot Gris is gradually assuming the mantle of 'chief white' from Chardonnay, thanks to greater aromatic pulling power. Things are changing, of course. Everything I have written above applies to the Willamette Valley, south of Portland. Now, though, wineries are beginning to speckle the warmer Umpqua and Rogue Valleys, closer to the Californian border. Oregon Cabernet is now viable.

Washington is a fierce, grand, faintly disturbing winegrowing environment. There are a few vines around rainy Seattle, but the vast majority of the state's vines lie 300 km or more from the moderating ocean. Winters always freeze and sometimes kill; summers burn. The rainfall is derisory, and the hills bare – until the drippers are turned on. It's high country: heat slithers away after dark like a rattlesnake. The result is a set of wines in which drama is engrained: a distant northern echo of Argentina's Mendoza. Expect deep colours, vivid acidity and forceful flavours. Chardonnay and Merlot blaze the trail, with Syrah, Cabernet and Riesling galloping along behind. Cowboys didn't drink wine, but if they had…

Now let's head east. New York State's Finger Lakes have a long winegrowing history; two-thirds of the vines planted here are American natives or hybrids. Riesling and Chardonnay, though, can be teased into viability. Long Island is a newer discovery: North Fork and the Hamptons melt into the Atlantic with a softness which recalls the Médoc. (Perhaps we should not be surprised: Long Island is on Istanbul's latitude.) Bordeaux varieties flourish over a long season here, making civilized wines.

The fact that Virginia is today the fifth most *vinifera*-populous state in the Union would thrill Thomas Jefferson, who laboured so hard against all odds to duplicate Pauillac at Monticello. The phylloxera which floored his efforts is now defeated, but Virginia's boisterous subtropical climate remains a big challenge. Light, lively but petite wines reward the victors.

Fine wines Fine wines in the USA fall into three categories. The first category is that of the grandees: sometimes old-established vineyards in classic areas, especially the Napa Valley, with a proven track record of ageing. The second category is that of the 'terroiristes': those working unremittingly to coax profundity from distinguished sites, wherever they may be found. And the third category is that of the cult wine: individuals or estates whose wines have been garlanded with dazzling point scores, most notably by Robert Parker. There are great wines in every category (and some overlap, of course, between them); great value, by contrast, is most likely to be found in the middle category, especially among those just beginning to win renown.

Fun wines The sheer number of wineries competing in the American market means that there is plenty of fun to be had by the curious consumer. Look out, in particular, for wines from less well-known grape varieties (like white Arneis or Marsanne, or red Petite Syrah) and wines from newly established wineries in fast-changing regions like Washington State or California's Central Coast. Avoid big brands, where the fun is often laboured.

National strengths Exuberance, warmth and breadth of flavour, combined with a passion for the discovery of new sites, new expressions and new levels of achievement.

National weaknesses An occasional love of power for its own sake among fine-wine producers. Sweetness and blandness in big-brand wines.

Canada

TRY Comparing a German Eiswein with a Canadian icewine would be an expensive exercise: a sip of either is a rare treat. Don't expect great subtlety, but enjoy the unique sensations.

TRY Ontario Chardonnay is one of those wines with which to tease your wine-loving friends in blind tastings: their weight and restraint seem almost European, yet there is something about their use of oak and their flavour repertoire that is distinctively different.

WHAT PEOPLE LOVE ABOUT

Canadian Wines
+ The fact that they exist at all.
+ The sensational quality of the icewines.
+ The restraint, freshness and food-friendliness of the better dry white and red wines.

OPPOSITE A frozen bunch of half-rotten grapes may not look very promising, but just wait until you taste the resulting icewine. Thus winter completes summer's work.

Two provinces dominate Canada's wine production, and both rely on water in order to flourish. Not so much for irrigation (though Canada does, like Washington State, grow some of its vines on desert land); more for the ability of water to temper Canada's intemperate winter weather. Even so, the one wine style which has made Canada's name will surprise no one. It's icewine.

Ontario is the province with the most vineyards to its name (almost 18,000 acres – considerably more than Oregon in the USA). These vines are squeezed onto the narrow belt of land running west from the Niagara Falls, dividing Lake Erie to the south from Lake Ontario to the north. The great idling masses of water, in particular, store summer's heat long enough into autumn to ripen both the hybrid variety Vidal and *Vitis vinifera* wines, too. The Niagara escarpment and the differing temperatures of the lakes keep a play of breezes moving, combatting fungal diseases in summer and sheathing winter's fangs. Nonetheless, the regular winter freeze, arriving like a polar express from the north, makes what is a rare and occasional speciality in Germany into an annual occurrence in Canada.

Keep those grapes on the vine long enough, and every year will provide a harvest when the grapes clatter in the buckets. The watery part of their juice remains stone-hard, while its sour-sweet essence trickles into the vats, and its scent fills the cold cellar air with lost summer. The resulting icewines twitch

with an electric jolt of sweetness and acidity. Canada makes red icewine, too.

There are more vines on the north shore of Lake Erie, and new vineyards spreading along the north shore of Lake Ontario, too, in the limestones of Prince Edward County. (The vines on the south side of Lake Erie are American.) Ontario is more than simply an icewine producer, as these new vineyards mean to prove: Pinot Noir, Syrah and Cabernet Franc can all thrive here. Chardonnay, though, has been the most successful variety for Ontario's table wines so far, occasionally achieving the kind of taut resonance that defines white burgundy.

It's a long journey west to British Columbia, where the inland Okanagan Valley, threading its way down towards the border, accomplishes in the Rockies what Lake Geneva does in the Alps: it provides enough warmth and reflected light, in other words, to bring Chardonnay, Merlot, Gewurztraminer and other *vinifera* varieties to a cool, brisk and refreshing maturity. The Okanagan style tends to be fruitier and more exuberant than that of Ontario. There are more vineyards in nearby Similkameen Valley, while out on Vancouver Island an array of hybrid exotica joins Pinot Gris and Pinot Noir in sitting out a teasing, testing summer. If you're buying wine in Canada, by the way, make sure you read the small print on the label: many ostensibly local wines are in fact blends of imported wine and local wine (which merely claim to be 'cellared in Canada').

Fine wines Great icewine,
especially when based on
Riesling. Some Syrah,
Bordeaux blends and
Chardonnay show promise.

Fun wines Everything else.

National strengths Freshness
and vivacity.

National weaknesses The
worst icewines can be vulgar
and coarse; the worst *vinifera*
wines can be strangely flavoured
and hollow.

**PROJECT 14
PLACES:
South America
and Mexico**

Few places in the modern world seem as predestined to make wine, given the clemency of their climates and their great reservoir of snowy water, as Chile and Argentina. Only the easy vineyards have been planted so far: deep loams, bright sun, irrigation by mere gravity. Now the era of difficult vineyards is beginning: stony hillsides, cooler climates, dry farming. Who knows what grandeur lies ahead?

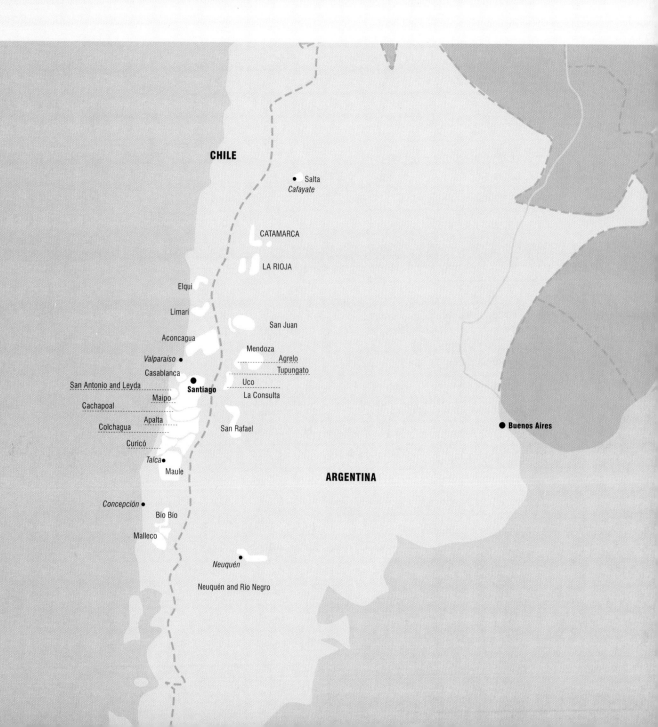

Chile

Chile is a gifted child. Of all the world's wine nations, none has the inherent aptitude for viticulture which central Chile does. Vines grow easily here, under blue skies of monotonous beauty; they have few disease problems; and the resulting wines have a kind of round-contoured affability to them, with intrinsically sweet fruit and pillow-feather tannins, which makes them hard to dislike. That has been Chile's story so far. The plains under the Andes between Santiago and Concepción are a factory for Cabernet Sauvignon of blackcurranty charm and Merlot full of elusive softness. Value and pleasure: what else do you want?

Well, fresh whites would be nice. It was Chile's quest for whites to match its lovely reds that began to change things. The search led, from 1982, to the novel planting of the Casablanca Valley, between Santiago and the sea port of Valparaíso. Too cool, the cynics said. (Why? Remember California and its cold, fog-forming ocean? Chile, too, is swept by cold ocean currents: coastal means cool.) Too dry, the accountants said (no Andes meltwater here; just expensive boreholes). But the quality of Casablanca's Chardonnay and Sauvignon Blanc soon persuaded both they'd been wrong. Lettuces once ruled Casablanca. No more.

Since then, Chile has been expanding its repertoire, often to highly impressive effect. We all know about the Andes, but only those who visit Chile will discover a second, older and more heavily eroded chain of mountains called the Coastal Ranges. Planting on the ocean side of the Coastal Ranges provides very cool conditions (look out for Leyda and San Antonio); planting on the land side brings more stoniness and subtlety to Chile's warm flesh. The boulder-strewn slopes of the Andes, too, are now being explored for winegrowing. To north and south, difficult gambles are paying off. In the north, high-sited Limarí and Elqui produce wines of intrinsic drama: cool nights bring bracing balance. In the south, Bío-Bío and Malleco tease varieties like Pinot Noir, Chardonnay and Riesling towards cool, taut nuance. Taut? Chile? Everything's changing.

Varietally speaking, the country's growing up, too. The fact that much of what was once considered Merlot has proved to be an old Bordeaux variety called Carmenère, packed with dark, brisk, creamy-smooth fruits, is another gift to Chile: a variety to call its own. Every serious wine-producing country needs a Pinot quest; Chile now has one, and the results are encouraging. Syrah (unsurprisingly, given that so many of Chile's soils are formed of decomposed granite) has surged. Some of the coutry's most ambitious wines, meanwhile, are now blends, in which the best flat-land old-vine material can enjoy a fling with younger, newer, higher-planted vines. The result is that the sweet fruit which is Chile's birthright is now ballasted by something deeper, chewier and more serious. Finally, weather models suggest that Chile may be less adversely affected by global warming than rival southern-hemisphere nations. Keep sampling Chile.

TRY Compare a Casablanca Sauvignon Blanc with one from New Zealand's Marlborough: which is the subtler and more satisfying wine?

TRY Compare the brambly fruits and low acidity of a good varietal Carmenère with brighter, crunchier Cabernet Sauvignon. (Neither, by the way, should have a green, leafy quality – a common Chilean failing.)

TRY Compare a red wine from Limarí with one from Maipo or Colchagua. The former will have a zingier balance; the latter pair will be softer and fuller.

WHAT PEOPLE LOVE ABOUT

Chilean Wines

+ The soft textures and sweet fruit of the red wines.
+ The increasing liveliness and poise of the whites.
+ Their good nature and friendliness.
+ Their value for money.

OPPOSITE ABOVE LEFT New, cool-climate sites have given birth to Chile's first great whites, led by the Casablanca Valley.

OPPOSITE ABOVE RIGHT Those hills are the challenge for the future. Harder work to cultivate – but maybe they'll produce world-beating wines?

OPPOSITE BELOW Errazuriz vines, basking in the Aconcagua Valley sunshine below cross and cactus.

Argentina

Argentina is a kind of vinous Tibet: vines, here, grow as close to the roof of the world as they ever will. The average height of the country's vineyards is 900 metres, and the loftiest ripen their grapes at over 3,000 metres. Don't, though, imagine anything Alpine: the typical Argentine vineyard is almost beach-flat, on deep sand and loam. These are sheltered depositional shelves and benches under the Andean peaks, which glimmer snowily on the horizon like a mirage. Viticulture is only possible at this height because the latitude is so low. A northern-hemisphere equivalent? Imagine vineyards nestling in North Africa's Atlas Mountains. (Maybe they will one day.)

Can you taste height in wine? Yes – and you can see it, too. The dashing purple-black of many Argentine reds, combined with their vivid acid balances, is a legacy of the cool nights which invariably temper daytime excesses. Temperatures drop by 20°C (36°F) at night. Cloudless skies and clear air during the summer days, though, send ripeness levels soaring, and few serious Argentinian wines finish fermenting at less than 13.5% or 14% abv. Rainfall levels are pitiful; irrigation is always necessary. Nor is the growing season quite as serene here as in Chile. Spring nights can be dangerously frosty and, on some summer afternoons, apocalyptic thunderheads gather over the Andes like migraines in the sky. The resulting hail can slash a vineyard to shreds in minutes. At its best, however, the risks are more than worth it: Argentina's finest reds have a poise, dignity and gastronomic logic to them that is rare in the southern hemisphere. It is significant that there has been more inward investment from Bordeaux to Argentina's Mendoza region than to any other southern-hemisphere location.

Mendoza, indeed, is Argentina's Bordeaux: 70% of the country's vineyards are here. Great vineyards lie close to the city itself, sometimes on gravels as well as alluvium and sand; another increasingly important zone is the Uco Valley to the south of the city. Luján de Cuyo, Agrelo, Tupungato, Vista Flores, La Consulta: not bullfighters, not tango dancers, but Mendozan sub-regions battling for reputation.

Three other provinces, far from Mendoza, offer something different. Northerly Salta is Argentina's highest region: its best reds are dark, salty, almost troublingly intense, and its white Torrontés is some of the country's most fragrant. Pitched in the deep south, where the continent dissolves into the cold and fury of Cape Horn, lie the vineyards of Argentina's Patagonia: Neuquén and Río Negro. Expect less flesh on the bones, and less of an alcoholic glow on the wines' cheeks. Instead, look for fine-grained fruit.

Malbec is Argentina's red-grape hero, but Bonarda, Sangiovese, Barbera and Tempranillo are all widely planted, as well as the ubiquitous Cabernet and Merlot. Pinot Noir (or Negro) is promising in Patagonia. Whites are less well-established in this steak-eating culture, apéritif Torrontés aside, but great efforts have gone into Chardonnay.

TRY Compare Mendoza Malbec with France's Cahors: vivacious fruit is more likely to be prominent in the Argentine version, and stony depths in the French.

TRY Argentina's grape mix lets you make comparisons between Argentine Sangiovese and Italy's Chianti, as well as between Argentine Tempranillo and Spain's Ribera del Duero.

TRY Compare a Torrontés from Salta with a dry Muscat from the Vins de Pays d'Oc: which has more perfume? And which offers more palate satisfaction?

WHAT PEOPLE LOVE ABOUT

Argentinian Wines
+ The vivacity and depth of the greatest Malbecs.
+ Their wide range of red grape varieties.
+ The mealtime aptitude of the red wines.
+ Their value for money.

OPPOSITE A Bordeaux dream in distant Mendoza: these are the vineyards of the freshly prospected Clos de los Siete, high in the Uco Valley, where Pomerol know-how is working on arid, sub-Andean wilderness.

The Rest of South America and Mexico

Only one South American nation lies entirely south of the Tropic of Capricorn: Uruguay. Low, humid and maritime, conditions here are very different to the high desert vineyards of Argentina or Chile's winegrowing garden of Eden. Its leading grape variety is different, too: Tannat (alias Harriague) first travelled here with Basque emigrants, and settled with them, too. The results are juicier and less tough than in France's Madiran, and the variety blends happily with others, especially Merlot.

Most of Brazil's vineyards lie just north of the Uruguayan border. Drenching rainfall encouraged, historically, the planting of hybrids, but by siting vineyards as far south as possible or, failing that, on high hills further north, the classic varieties are beginning to speak Brazilian Portuguese. In tropical Brazil (as in Thailand), careful management of some rather confused vines succeeds in producing two crops a year of passable winemaking fruit.

The only other South American nation whose wines rise above curiosity status is Peru. They may lie on the same latitude as Addis Ababa, but thanks to the Humboldt current and the resulting coastal fogs and breezes, viticulture is possible. Muscat grapes destined for distillation into pisco (the aromatic white mixing brandy of Chile, Peru and Bolivia, named after the city of the same name on Peru's coast) dominate production, but the usual repertoire of varietal wines is making headway.

Back to the northern hemisphere, finally. Like Peru, Mexico is predominantly a brandy-producing country. The long tongue of Baja California is (thanks to those cold currents again) better suited to winegrowing than its latitude would suggest, and Mexico can produce some impressively sturdy reds from Petite Syrah and Nebbiolo, as well as the more familiar international varieties.

Fine wines Twenty years ago, South America had none. Now, both Chilean and Argentinian producers like to top their ranges with lavishly flavoured 'icon wines'. These are usually blends, bottled in heavy glass and ambitiously priced. Some are overworked and, while impressive, laborious to drink; others (especially those based on old-vine fruit) hint at true grandeur and profundity. It is, however, regional (or vineyard) origin and market demand which will create the icon wines of the future. Chile's profile will continue to be aromatically charming, round-contoured, soft and seductive; Argentina's reds will remain deeper, denser and more muscular.

Fun wines Look for many fine-value examples of the key varietals from each country: Cabernet Sauvignon and Carmenère from Chile, and Malbec and Torrontés from Argentina. More recently planted Syrah, too, is flourishing in both countries, and whites are improving fast. Look out, too, for deep-coloured rosé wines from both Chile and Argentina.

National strengths Richness, generosity, softness of balance and value.

National weaknesses Chile's worst red wines are marked by grassy, herbaceous characters, and the whites by a simple, confected style. Argentina's worst wines are coarsely made and crude in style, often with stinky 'reduced' characters.

**PROJECT 15
PLACES:
Australia**

Australia trains the world's most scientifically literate winemakers. No one markets wine more effectively than Australians. Given adequate water, much of the continent is suitable for trouble-free, mechanized viticulture. Australia has some of the earth's oldest vines, giving reds of unparalleled intensity. The country's recent success has been built on these four foundations. Great vineyards, though, are the future.

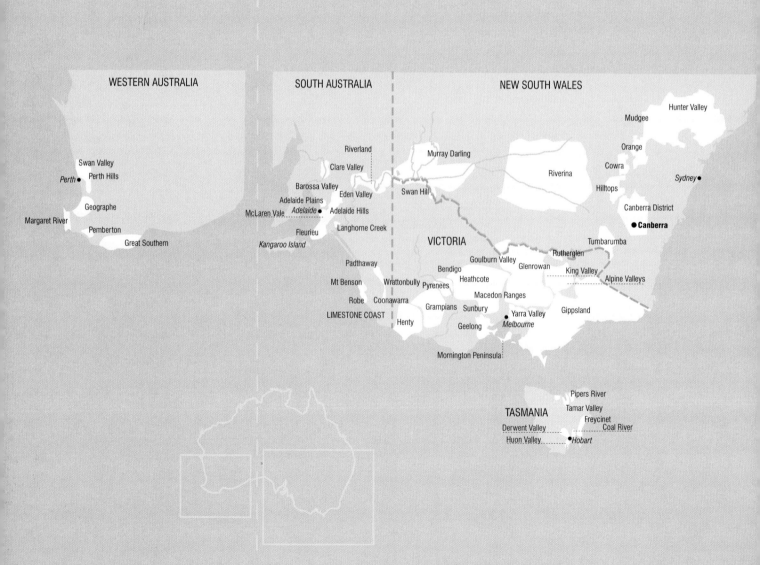

WESTERN AUSTRALIA

Swan Valley
Perth • Perth Hills

Geographe

Margaret River

Pemberton

Great Southern

SOUTH AUSTRALIA

Riverland

Clare Valley

Barossa Valley
Adelaide Plains
McLaren Vale   Adelaide • Eden Valley
Adelaide Hills
Fleurieu   Langhorne Creek
Kangaroo Island

Padthaway

Mt Benson   Wrattonbully
Robe   Coonawarra
LIMESTONE COAST

NEW SOUTH WALES

Hunter Valley
Mudgee

Orange
Murray Darling   Cowra
Riverina
Swan Hill   Hilltops   Sydney •

Canberra District
● Canberra

VICTORIA   Tumbarumba
Rutherglen
Goulburn Valley
Bendigo   Glenrowan   King Valley   Alpine Valleys
Heathcote
Macedon Ranges
Pyrenees
Grampians   Sunbury   Gippsland
Henty   Geelong   Yarra Valley
•   Melbourne

Mornington Peninsula

Pipers River
TASMANIA   Tamar Valley
Freycinet
Derwent Valley   Coal River
Huon Valley   • Hobart

Victoria

Australia is an empty continent with a crowded coastline. Of the country's five mainland states, Victoria is the smallest – and the most southerly, the wettest and the most densely populated. The Great Dividing Range strides north from Victoria. There are no ghastly blanks here; the countryside is peaceful, gum-strewn but busy, with some 60% of the land surface farmed. Vineyards punctuate sheep paddocks and wheat fields. In Australian terms, it's the home of the small grower. Neighbouring South Australia may produce twice as much wine, but it has half as many wineries.

Out of this mosaic of winegrowing, regional characters and styles are slowly beginning to emerge. Beginning? One emerged back in the gold-rush days of the nineteenth century: the sweet fortified wines (or 'stickies') of Rutherglen and Glenrowan in the state's hot north, growing along the banks of the River Murray and marking Victoria's border with New South Wales. They remain a world original: tin-shed titans made from Muscat and Muscadelle, smoothed by heat and cask years into unctuous grandeur. South of the Murray, the land begins to rise towards the Victorian Alps: Beechworth is the home of some of Australia's most accomplished Chardonnays, and King Valley a centre for innovative varietal planting.

The Goulburn Valley, Heathcote, the Pyrenees and the Grampians: soil types vary greatly as rumpled Victoria spreads westward, and so, too, do climatic nuances, depending on altitude and orientation. The Shiraz that you will find from these regions doesn't have the sweet power and amplitude which defines Shiraz in South Australia's Barossa Valley or McLaren Vale, but it more than makes up for it in terms of subtlety, nuance and truth to place. The best of these, for me, are lodestar Australian reds: complex, allusive and balanced, full of the scents of the bush as the long, hot day unburdens into night. Rich, mallowy white Marsanne is another speciality.

A move south and increments of height mean lower temperatures – to the extent that many of the finest sparkling-wine raw materials in Australia are sourced from Victoria's coolest spots, such as southerly Henty or the Strathbogie and Macedon Ranges just north of Melbourne. The vineyard halo around the city, finally, is the place to look for some of Australia's most finely sculpted Pinot Noir and Chardonnay. Geelong across Port Phillip Bay, the sea-washed jawbone of the Mornington Peninsula and, above all, the undulating Yarra Valley to the city's north-east constitute, at present, a kind of dislocated Australian Côte d'Or, their best wines poised and vivacious. Shiraz (increasingly blended with a little Viognier) and sparkling wines are other Yarra specialities. Non-Australians sometimes assume that every wine the country produces must be throbbing like a roadtrain. If you want to discover a lighter, fresher and more poised Australia, head for Melbourne.

TRY Compare Pinot Noir from the Mornington Peninsula or the Yarra Valley with Pinot Noir from both New Zealand and Burgundy. Much depends on vintage and producer, but in many cases the Victorian examples will be midway between the fruited charm of New Zealand and the pungency, sinew and edge of the Burgundy.

TRY Compare a Marsanne from Victoria with a Marsanne-dominated blend from France's northern Rhône: the Australian version is likely to be more exuberant, deeper and more characterful, while the French examples will generally be suppler, softer and subtler.

TRY Compare a fine Shiraz from Heathcote, the Pyrenees or the Grampians with an equivalently priced example from South Australia's Barossa or McLaren Vale. See which you prefer without food – and then over the course of a meal. With food and time, the Victorian wine may impress most, though perhaps not initially.

WHAT PEOPLE LOVE ABOUT

Victorian Wines

+ The balance and individuality of Victorian Shiraz.
+ The freshness and poise of the Chardonnay and Pinot Noir.
+ The remarkable value and quality of the sparkling wines.
+ The magnificent concentration and personality of the stickies.

OPPOSITE A moist start to the Yarra summer. The Yeringberg vineyards won the region nineteenth-century fame.

South Australia

TRY South Australia provides a rainbow spectrum of Shiraz: compare the richness of Barossa and McLaren Vale with the peppery purity of Clare Valley and the mineral force of Mount Barker.

TRY Compare Cabernet from Coonawarra with Cabernet from Napa to prove that Australia doesn't have to mean massive.

TRY A Riesling from Clare Valley or Eden Valley with a salad lunch: it's a great food match.

TRY One of South Australia's remarkable sparkling Shiraz wines: a world original, and implausibly good.

WHAT PEOPLE LOVE ABOUT

South Australian Wines

* The lush, extravagant, sweet-fruited generosity of Barossa and McLaren Vale Shiraz.
* The fine-scented, curranty purity of Cabernet and Merlot from Coonawarra and Wrattonbully.
* The tropical fruits, dry pungency and mineral dignity of Riesling from the Eden Valley and, especially, the Clare Valley.
* The finesse and elegance of wines from the Adelaide Hills.

OPPOSITE Perennially dry hills worry winegrowers in South Australia, where enduring drought is the biggest threat.

This is Australia's wine state, crushing almost half the nation's grapes every year. Such is the scale of Australia, though, that all this activity is confined to a fragment of the state's landmass: a spatter of wine regions clustered around its capital, Adelaide. ('South-Eastern Australia', by contrast, covers 98% of all Australian vineyard land, with only Western Australia excluded.)

Think of Australia, and you think of the Barossa Valley. Australia's biggest quality wine region lies north-east of Adelaide. 'Valley', here, doesn't mean the tumbling drama of Germany's Mosel, France's Côte Rôtie or Portugal's Douro; at best, there's a soft roll to the vineyards, with the fringing hills no bigger than a single pillow at a bed's end. Deep loams and sand; bright, dry warmth; and 100-year-old Shiraz vines form the core of Barossa's appeal. The long, cossetting season seems to bring fruit here to unrivalled ripeness which, often combined with the aromatic sweetness of American oak, makes black-red wine of almost treacly textures and sensationally lush flavours. The Eden Valley lies next door – but is notably higher and windier, with more gravel in the sand and loam. The Shiraz is fresher and more singing in style, and Riesling thrives here, making dry, strong, pure wines which age well. The stonier Clare Valley, to the north-west of Barossa and Eden, produces outstandingly perfumed, poised and structured Riesling; indeed for me these are Australia's finest white wines. Savoury Shiraz and Cabernet add to the Clare's attractions.

Adelaide itself has both Hills and Plains. The two are very different. The Plains are hot and loamy; the Hills cool enough to produce Chardonnay of elegance and poise, and fine base wine for sparkling wines. The Hills drop away through fine Sauvignon Blanc country from Mount Lofty down towards Mount Barker, where some of Australia's most Rhône-like Shiraz comes into being. Eventually the region shades into the much warmer though breeze-affected McLaren Vale, whose monster Shiraz can out-sumo that of the Barossa. Juicy Grenache and chocolatey Cabernet are other specialities. Langhorne Creek, stretching back from the shores of Lake Alexandrina, is home to more rich reds, while the Fleurieu Peninsula and Kangaroo Island, tapering into the Southern Ocean, are still in their formative years. Their maritime mildness promises much.

Coonawarra, far to the south of Adelaide, with neighbouring regions like Wrattonbully, Padthaway and Mount Benson, form an expanding 'Limestone Coast'. Red soil over white, limey calcrete, combined with cool growing conditions, create scented, brisk, lean-line Cabernet and Merlot as well as (in warm vintages) truly vivacious yet savoury Shiraz: those are the Coonawarra hallmarks. Wrattonbully offers a more expansive reading. Finally, much further north at the point at which the River Murray ambles into South Australia, lies 'Riverland', where around a quarter of Australia's grapes are grown every year, irrigation allowing. This is brand-fuel for the big companies. Juicy jollity is the aim.

The Rest of Australia

The bright, friendly magnet of Sydney means that many visitors' exposure to Australian wine begins and ends in the Hunter Valley, to the north of the city. That fun day out (lunch, golf, the lot) is both peculiar and appropriate. Peculiar in that, as a winegrowing area, the Hunter Valley shouldn't exist: most of its generous rainfall comes as the fruit is ripening, and no one need plant subtropical vineyards in a country so amply blessed, elsewhere, with dry summers. If the Hunter wasn't so near Sydney, they wouldn't have.

In another sense, though, it's appropriate: Australia is the world leader in cross-regional blending, and a sizeable minority of the wine sold by wineries in the Hunter began life as fruit growing elsewhere. Rich, lactic Chardonnay and spiky, mid-weight Shiraz are genuinely indigenous, as is the distinctive Hunter Valley Semillon. Picked unripe, it makes dull drinking when young, but ages towards something oddly yet compellingly characterful. There are coastal vineyards to the north and south of Sydney (Hastings River and the Shoalhaven Coast respectively), but their little-exported wines struggle in the teeth of damp summers.

It's up on the heights of the Great Dividing Range where the fine-wine future of New South Wales probably lies. Mudgee is, the Hunter aside, NSW's oldest region: the evocative Aboriginal name means 'nest in the hills'. It's happily drier and cooler than the Hunter. That climate and the region's loams produce a set of mid-weight Australian classics. Cowra to the south is lower-lying: buttery Chardonnay is a speciality. Nearby Hilltops is mainly known for grape-supplying rather than wine-bottling, as is remote, mountainous, super-cool Tumbarumba: fruit from the latter serves to brace some of the big companies' top sparkling-wine and white-wine ranges, and few doubt that we'll see great single-vineyard whites from here in due course. Orange, meanwhile, is high and windy, reflected in a range of fresh, elegant reds and whites where exact site and soil type are more than usually important.

The Australian Capital Territory, created in the early twentieth century to silence squabbles between Sydney and Melbourne, has defied its reputation as a dull hive of civil servants with some disconcertingly good Rhône-style Shiraz (some of it given an exciting swirl of Viognier); Pinot Noir and Riesling have also surprised. Politics means that most of the vineyard land lies outside the ACT border: only leasehold ownership is possible inside, hence the name 'Canberra District' – with the emphasis on District.

In terms of quantity, though, New South Wales means Riverina, Swan Hill and the Murray Darling: upstream echoes of South Australia's Riverland. Heat, irrigation and mechanization fill millions of cases a year, though the ever-present threats of drought and land salination may eventually check this industrious landscape.

Western Australia, an odyssey away from the rest of the country, produces a small single-figure percentage of the national wine

TRY Compare a Cabernet from Margaret River with one from Coonawarra. Coonawarra's may have more aromatic purity, but the Margaret River example may be an easier and more satisfying drink. Try blending the two yourself, in best Australian spirit.

TRY Look out for Chardonnay from Orange, Chardonnay from the Adelaide Hills and Chardonnay from Tasmania: which do you think might disconcert Burgundians most?

TRY Compare sparkling wine from Tasmania with Champagne. You may find more fruit flavours in the Tasmanian wine, but more creamy finesse in the Champagne. Note, though, the similar balance and cut of the wines.

TRY Compare Pinot Noir from Tasmania with Pinot Noir from the Yarra Valley, and try to tease out the differences.

OPPOSITE Zinfandel leaves and ironstone pebbles make a Western Australian autumn sonata. By now the wines will be safely stowed in vats and barrels.

Western Australian Wines

✦ Their delicacy and potential for understatement, qualities still unusual in the Australian context.

✦ The balance, drinkability and potential for ageing of the Cabernets and Cabernet-Merlot blends.

✦ The layered quality of the best Chardonnays.

✦ Fresh citrus and tropical fruits in the blended whites.

Tasmanian Wines

✦ The freshness and incisiveness of the sparkling wines.

✦ The unforced purity, freshness and poise of the best Pinot Noirs.

✦ The surprising success of Cabernet and Merlot from the warmest vineyard sites.

OPPOSITE Pristine Tasmania. These sparkling-wine vines in Pipers Brook photosynthesize the sunlight which cascades through the world's most unpolluted vineyard air – and it shows. Holding fruit flavours in check is the challenge.

total, but is disproportionately represented at the top table for medals, superlatives and auction stardust. Margaret River is its leading region, best known for Cabernet. Forget the piercing acidity and arrowhead focus of Coonawarra: the climate here is of nurse-like gentleness, with sea breezes and mild winters (during which the vines sleep only reluctantly) the biggest challenge. The result is warm, settled wines with enduring internal architecture but a distinctively Australian, sweetly savoury flavour. Are the presence of gravel, and temperatures very close to those of Bordeaux in a good vintage, reasons why Margaret River Cabernet ages so well? Maybe. Chardonnay runs Cabernet a close second: it's ample and multi-layered. Sauvignon Blanc, Semillon and Chenin Blanc all blend with unusual contentment into bright, lime-fresh whites, and Semillon works better as a varietal wine here than anywhere else in the country. Margaret River Shiraz, meanwhile, is more spice girl than sumo wrestler, with medium-weight fruit.

Wineries are scattered about the rest of Western Australia as sparsely as islands in the Pacific, which makes generalizations about their styles difficult. Most, though, are within an hour or two of the vast masses of the Southern Ocean (next stop, Antarctica) and the Indian Ocean (next stop, Madagascar), and that maritime proximity means mild winters and warm rather than hot summers. Their print is an overall delicacy in the wines without over-strict rules about grape variety: in the sub-regions of the vast zone known as Great Southern, you can find pithy Riesling, peppery Shiraz, fragrant Pinot and tropical Verdelho.

Confident Perth itself, meanwhile, is much hotter than the breezy south; indeed the Swan Valley is one of Australian wine's hottest spots (no wonder the swans are black). It has had an oddly glorious white-wine past, but its future may be Hunter-like: welcoming day-tripping tourists, and pouring them wines made from grapes grown somewhere else altogether.

Yes, Queensland does have vineyards, most of them clustered around Brisbane. Most promising, though, is the Granite Belt region on the New South Wales border, winning a name for its dark and forceful Shiraz and Cabernet wines, picked late in the season.

Tasmania's potential, though, is far greater, though its geographical complexities and challenges mean that vineyard evolution is in its early stages. Raw geography would suggest a white-wine and sparkling-wine vocation, yet fine Australian Cabernet, full of nuanced ripeness, is grown in the Coal River Valley in southern Tasmania. Somewhere or other, almost anything seems possible on this intricate, jewel-like island, especially when the varietal repertoire expands a little (what would Petit Manseng, Grüner Veltliner or Furmint be like here?). Sensibly, though, it is Pinot Noir, sparkling wine and aromatic whites that dominate plantings in both northern and southern Tasmania during these pioneering years. Wind, frost and rain put a premium on sheltered sites when it comes to bringing varieties destined for non-sparkling wines to full ripeness: look out for the Tamar Valley, the Coal River Valley and the Freycinet amphitheatre for the ripest Pinot and expectation-defying Cabernet and Merlot.

FACT FILE: Australia

Fine wines International attention has focused on Australia's biggest reds, many from the Barossa Valley and McLaren Vale, and based on old-vine fruit, exuberant winemaking extractions and lavish use of American as well as French oak rather than precise vineyard origin. Note, too, that Australia is the only country whose finest wines include examples (such as Penfold's celebrated Grange) made by blending the fruit of different regions. Increasingly, though, it is single-vineyard and small-grower wines of more delicate style which are winning renown, and the search for distinguished vineyard sites is now key for many working to create Australia's finest wines.

Fun wines Australia's ocean of branded, big-company wine is all based on the fun principle, and there are many indigenous styles (like the country's sparkling Shiraz wines and stickies) that combine grandeur with fun in a uniquely Australian way. Perhaps, too, the appeal of Australia's richest reds is that, unlike much 'fine wine', they offer the drinker a lot of eye-popping, tongue-thumping, tonsil-staining fun.

National strengths
Exuberance, increasing variety, value, consistency.

National weaknesses
Many Australian reds are marred by exaggerated acid additions, and the importance accorded to technical winemaking parameters in the country's wineries mean that many wines are samey. Regional or site characteristics can be 'corrected' away in the winemaking process. Viticulture can be inadequately fastidious.

PROJECT 16
PLACES:
New Zealand

Two lush, green stone ships on an 80-million-year journey into the Pacific: that's New Zealand. It's lucky. No southern-hemisphere rival has a white-wine vocation. None has created a world original out of Sauvignon Blanc. None has discovered that its red grape of choice is the much-courted but often disdainful Pinot Noir. Wool, lamb and cheap butter once summed up the country. Wine has made New Zealand sexy.

North Island

New Zealand's North Island was where the country's vineyards were pioneered (by a missionary named Marsden), just seven years after Napoleon's retreat from Moscow – though serious efforts had to wait for the arrival of Dalmatian and Lebanese immigrants a century later. Auckland itself, and the Northland region which stretches to the tip of the North Island, aren't ideal for winegrowing; like Australia's Hunter Valley, subtropical heat and summer rain vex winegrowers. In contrast to the Hunter Valley, though, care and attention can help produce Chardonnay of unique sumptuousness within the New Zealand context in these areas. The driest spots (which in New Zealand nearly always means the furthest east) are also capable of making Cabernet Sauvignon and Merlot wines without the grassiness which has bedevilled other Kiwi efforts with these varieties. Waiheke Island, a ferry-ride from the capital, is one of the best spots in the country to discover balanced, forthright Bordeaux blends and Syrah-based reds. Matakana and Cleveland on the nearby mainland are promising, too. A little further south, Waikato (or the Bay of Plenty) is producing exuberant Chardonnay – though it is Gisborne, further east, where many of New Zealand's winemakers look first and foremost for their Chardonnay. Late summer and autumn rain can still be troublesome here, but ample summer warmth swings the fruit towards a generous, custard-cream ripeness. Gewurztraminer of unusually convincing character is another asset.

Hawkes Bay once looked like New Zealand wine's safest bet – until the incandescent ascent of Marlborough in the South Island. It remains the country's second-largest wine area, as well as the one whose internal soil and climate variations permit the greatest range of expressive possibilities in its wines. Finely sculpted and fashioned Chardonnay is most planted, but much of the recent attention has focused on Pinot Gris, Merlot and Syrah. And on the 'Gimblett gravels': a former river bed, abandoned after violent flooding a century and a half ago, which aroused the interest of those familiar with the great beaches of gravel in Bordeaux's Médoc. The results are promising – but there are 21 other categories of soil type in Hawkes Bay, suggesting that there is much exciting evolution ahead.

Martinborough, at the south-eastern end of the island, was New Zealand's pioneering Pinot region. The broader area is now known as Wellington, and Martinborough itself has become a zone within Wellington's only official wine district, which is Wairarapa. (Maybe France isn't so complicated after all.) The climate is teasingly cool, especially at night; the game is possible thanks to long, dry autumn weather, while those intriguing gravels are a soil theme here, too. Wairarapa Pinots don't have the instant charm of those from Central Otago, but the best have a grain and a dark-fruited depth which lends them real distinction. Both Sauvignon Blanc and Pinot Gris provide white-wine diversion.

TRY A Chardonnay from Kumeu, near Auckland, and compare it with one from Gisborne and one from Hawkes Bay. You may find vivacity and poise in the Hawkes Bay wine; rich, lemon-cream fruit from Gisborne and layered textures in the Auckland example.

TRY Compare a Pinot Noir from Martinborough with a village red from Burgundy (such as Gevrey-Chambertin or Nuits-St Georges). Try to do it 'blind' (with the bottles wrapped in cooking foil or hidden in bags) and see if you can tell which is which.

TRY Compare a Sauvignon Blanc from any North Island region with one from Marlborough. Which one do you like best on its own? And which one with food?

WHAT PEOPLE LOVE ABOUT

Hawkes Bay Wines

+ The balance between refreshment and succulence in the Chardonnays.
+ The purity and vivacity of the Merlot (or Merlot-based blends) and Syrah wines, especially those grown on the Gimblett gravels.

Martinborough Wines

+ The dark-fruited, lithely structured yet approachable quality of the Pinot Noir.

OPPOSITE Pinot Noir and Sauvignon Blanc vines soak up the dazzle in Craggy Range's Te Muna Road vineyards near Martinborough. No wonder there's a piercing quality to New Zealand's best wines.

South Island

TRY One of the wine world's essential comparisons is Marlborough Sauvignon Blanc with Sancerre or Pouilly-Fumé (or even simple Sauvignon de Touraine) from France. Both are recognizably made from the same grape, and both should be memorable – but always in a different way. Compare two or three Marlborough Sauvignons, though, and you may find them difficult to tell apart. The same may be true of two or three Sancerres. Blame the grape.

TRY Good Pinot Noir from Central Otago demands to be compared to red Burgundy, too. There will usually be more evident fruit flavour in the Central Otago wine, but which one has most depth and finesse?

WHAT PEOPLE LOVE ABOUT

Marlborough Wines
+ The freshness, zinginess and pungency of the Sauvignon Blanc.
+ The edgy impact and depth of the Pinot Noir.
+ The promising quality of the sparkling wines.

Central Otago Wines
+ The energetic purity of fruit in the Pinot Noir.

OPPOSITE Sauvignon from the Cloudy Bay vineyards gets the latest in machine-harvesting technology – and some synchronized tractor-driving, too. Marlborough's explosive growth makes machines obligatory.

The first vine was planted in Marlborough in 1973. The region now produces over half of New Zealand's annual grape harvest. Nowhere in the wine world, in fact, proves the importance of what the French call *terroir* (see page 60) better than Marlborough. The grape variety which unlocked that potential was Sauvignon Blanc. What happened when Sauvignon met Marlborough? A kind of green explosion: pungently grassy scents and flavours, mingled with lime fruit, asparagus spears, a purée of gooseberries. Aromatic exuberance and flavoury vitality of this order could not be ignored, and can hardly be disliked. Nowhere else in the world can duplicate these conditions; nowhere else can grow Sauvignon that tastes exactly like this. Like a gold strike or an oil find, the prospecting of Marlborough Sauvignon has brought this former grazing region rapid prosperity. Unlike seams of metal ore and fossil-fuel reserves, though, it might endure. (Global warming makes even that uncertain.)

Is Marlborough good only for Sauvignon? In the early days, it may have seemed so. No longer. Leanly persuasive Chardonnay; streamlined Pinot Noir; finely tooled Riesling (with European-style orchard fruit as opposed to Australian-style tropical fruit); and excitingly complex sparkling wines based on that lean Chardonnay and streamlined Pinot are further reasons for the vineyard boom. Like Hawkes Bay, the soils are intriguingly various, with gravels an important subtext, and a move out of the main Wairau Valley to the slightly warmer Awatare Valley further south has opened a new chapter in what seems certain to prove a very long book.

Nelson, to Marlborough's west, is wetter and its wines have not yet been consistently successful, though its Riesling and Sauvignon can be very good; the vineyards of Canterbury, further south, are concentrated in two areas (cool Christchurch and warmer, limestone-soiled Waipara), and intermittently promising Pinot Noir and Chardonnay make both sub-regions worth a look.

If there is a rival for Marlborough, though, it is the beautiful region of Central Otago: lonely, majestic, pristine, the human thumbprint on the landscape still happily discreet. A long growing season and a warm, gentle autumn are typical (though not uniform) in maritime Marlborough; Central Otago, by contrast, lies underneath the mountains, and its continental summer is shorter. Shorter – but still more brilliant. The South Island's light has, at all times, a piercing, pristine, unpeeled quality that can bleach a fence-post in a single summer; in Central Otago, it is (literally: the ozone is thin here) blisteringly bright and hazeless. The result is Pinot Noir that seems to spurt from the bottle and splash in the glass. Another world-class *terroir*? Time must sign the warrant, but the early drafts are good. Central Otago's Pinot already has the kind of poise and comeliness which Burgundy finds hard to summon with any regularity; what's still missing is the inner musculature of stone and cool fire.

Fine wines The main drawback of New Zealand's success with Sauvignon Blanc is that it lacks one of the hallmarks of 'fine' wine: the ability to blossom over cellar years into something still more mellowly beautiful than it was in its youth. For that, the country looks to its Chardonnays, its Merlot-Cabernet blends, its top Syrah wines and its Pinot Noirs – though it is still in the experimental phase with all.

Fun wine Marlborough Sauvignon is fun from top to bottom, and the Gisborne style of Chardonnay is rarely long-faced, either. As a grape, Pinot Noir can be less fun than most – but not in New Zealand. A few stringy and herbaceous examples aside, fruit is generally well to the fore, and fruit puts the fun into Pinot.

National strengths Freshness, vivacity, vibrancy, cleanliness and energy.

National weaknesses New Zealand wines can be, quite literally, tediously good, and there is little for the lover of big, extractive reds.

PROJECT 17
PLACES:
South Africa

The lush quilt of green and gold is punctuated by rugged peaks of sandstone, or rounded granite plutons which bubble from the land. The clear air dissolves distance. The engine of evolution has worked itself to a floral frenzy here, leaving a legacy of 9,600 species. What of the wine vine? South Africa's fundamental advantage is that its wines lie poised between European elegance and southern-hemisphere generosity.

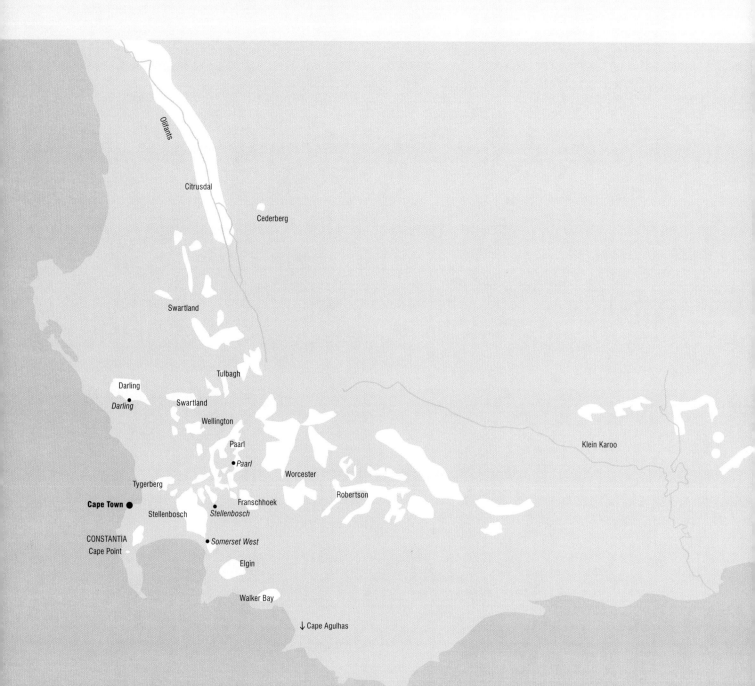

Olifants

Citrusdal

Cederberg

Swartland

Tulbagh

Darling
● Darling

Swartland

Wellington

Paarl
● Paarl

Worcester

Klein Karoo

Tygerberg

Robertson

Cape Town ●

Franschhoek

Stellenbosch   ● Stellenbosch

CONSTANTIA
Cape Point

● Somerset West

Elgin

Walker Bay

↓ Cape Agulhas

The Heartland

South Africa's history can be read in its landscape. Farms based on the land grants of the seventeenth century remain mostly unchanged today. Villages barely exist; black or coloured labour lodged on those white-owned farms until the end of the twentieth century. The stately grandeur of the landscape is built on this separation of humans by skin colour. Normal developmental chaos was kept at bay.

Winegrowing, like European settlement, radiated out from Cape Town, and the heartland of South Africa's wine industry remains a short drive from Table Mountain. Constantia is closest: the remnants of the farm of the Cape's second Dutch governor, Simon van der Stel. This is, literally, Table Mountain's back garden combined with the lee slope of Constantiaberg: a cool, cloudy, moist region where whites outnumber reds (Sauvignon Blanc and old-vine Semillon are both outstanding). The great dessert-wine tradition of the past, based on late-harvest Muscat, is maintained at Klein Constantia. Cape Point is even cooler and windier.

Stel's name lives on in Stellenbosch, the heart of the heartland, where Cape Town's scruffiest sprawl fades away into immaculate countryside. Paarl lies to the north of Stellenbosch and Somerset West to its south, set back from the waters of False Bay. Wine farms of epic splendour jostle each other here underneath a shepherd's crook of great peaks, enigmatically superintending the landscape. Proximity to the sea brings cool breezes, but most of this area is at least equivalent to Bordeaux in terms of summer warmth, and the exact position of a farm in relation to the mountains will always distinguish it from its neighbours. To the east of this region, the little valley of Franschhoek lies squeezed between three mountains in a glowing cul-de-sac. The lowest vineyards throughout the heartland are a mere 100 metres above sea level, while the mountain peaks can touch 1,700 metres: a recipe for drama. In 200 years, the potential of individual vineyards in this landscape may be understood as intimately as in the Médoc or Burgundy – but we're not there yet. Nor are South Africa's long-standing vine virus problems fully solved. Some farms (particularly in cramped Franschhoek) find fruit elsewhere, and blend at home.

What we might have to look forward to, though, can be tasted in the best wines. Bordeaux blends (both Cabernet-Merlot and Semillon-Sauvignon) of sometimes forceful but sometimes savoury, fragrant or creamy style are an undoubted strength, and a lot of effort has gone into Chardonnay, too, which can achieve confident sumptuousness here. Syrah or Shiraz is a newer passion, but the best look impressive whether as varietal wines or blends, especially from Wellington, north of Paarl. Two sorts of tradition are on offer in the Pinotage reds (at worst coarse and rubbery, at best vigorous, scented and deeply fruity) and the old-vine Chenin Blanc whites have chewy depth. Varietal Sauvignon needs a cool spot but can be good, the model being Graves rather than Loire.

TRY Compare Cabernet Sauvignon and Bordeaux blends from Stellenbosch with similar wines from the Napa Valley. The South African versions will usually be lighter and more graceful compared with the power and depth of California.

TRY Sauvignon Blanc from Constantia does not yet have the assurance of the best from New Zealand and vintage variation can be considerable, but its character profile at best has much of the same leafy, zingy charm.

TRY Two or three examples of Pinotage before you decide you don't like it. The best are unique: characterful, exuberant, refreshing and barbecue-friendly.

WHAT PEOPLE LOVE ABOUT

Heartland Wines

+ The innate complexity, balance and, sometimes, ageability of Bordeaux-blend reds from Stellenbosch and Paarl.
+ The fragrance and freshness of Constantia's white wines.
+ The excitement and character of old-vine Chenin Blanc and carefully vinified Pinotage.

OPPOSITE Paarl's hillside 'pearls' are in fact granite plutons. The vineyards feed on acid soils of weathered granite, just as they do in the northern Rhône – though the sun is more generous here.

The Diaspora

TRY Sauvignon Blanc from the Darling Hills, and compare it with Sauvignon Blanc from Elgin: the former generally has more charm, while the latter is leaner and sometimes deeper.

TRY Shiraz or red blends from top producers sourcing from Swartland, and compare their lazy, almost effortless warmth and complexity with the more polished, international styles of Stellenbosch.

TRY Chardonnay from Robertson: note its creamy fullness and easy varietal character.

TRY Walker Bay Chardonnay or Pinot Noir, and match them against French equivalents from Burgundy.

WHAT PEOPLE LOVE ABOUT

Diaspora Wines

+ New-wave Sauvignon from the Darling Hills and elsewhere.
+ The value for money of Robertson Chardonnay.
+ Impressive Shiraz, often in a Rhône rather than an Australian style.
+ The stylistic diversity and interest offered by regions like Swartland, Elgin and Walker Bay.
+ The quality of its hard-to-find fortified wines.

OPPOSITE Winter greenery at Groote Post in the Darling Hills, a sweet spot for fresh-flavoured Sauvignon Blanc.

In many ways, the story of South African wine in the early years of the twenty-first century is one of new discovery. Previously disdained or even unknown wine regions are suddenly winning wine competitions or unveiling dramatically good single-vineyard wines, and South Africa's law-makers are falling over themselves to catch up. The old, settled, Stellenbosch-centred wine universe is beginning to lose a little of its gravitational pull, surrounded by so many new satellites in flavoury orbit around it.

West of Stellenbosch lies Cape Town and the Atlantic; south of Stellebosch lies the Indian Ocean. Our diaspora, thus, lies north, north-east and south-east.

Swartland and its neighbouring districts, to the north of Cape Town, are old bulk-wine areas now revealing hidden secrets. Groenekloof in the Darling Hills is one: breezy, cool and beautiful, producing Sauvignon Blanc full of well-judged freshness. Tygerberg (Philadelphia and Durbanville) is another, for bright reds. But it is the warmth, comfort and complexity of Swartland's own reds, often dry-farmed (grown without aid of irrigation), as well as white blends with a high percentage of old-vine Chenin, which have brought out the terroiriste in many growers. Tasting these wines for the first time eerily recalls some of the ease and gentleness that marks the wines of France's Rhône Valley.

Tulbagh, a deep, broad trench hemmed in by mountains, can use its many different slopes and heights to create more Rhône-style reds as well as compelling Semillon. The tiny enclave of Cederberg, in a mountain fastness in the far north, illustrates that there is not just a world but a universe beyond Stellenbosch. Its racy whites and multi-layered reds, grown at over 1,000 metres, constitute a compelling incentive to the far flung.

And the north-east? This was the old trekking route up towards Kimberley, Johannesburg and Pretoria, so it is no surprise that the warm-to-hot wine regions here have some history to them. Worcester and Robertson are the main names. The former for volume: one-fifth of the Cape's grapes grow here, many of them for brandy production. Robertson, by contrast, produces fine Chardonnay and even Sauvignon. The disadvantages of climate here are remedied in part by long-distance sea breezes, but more significantly by vine-friendly limestone. Travel further north-east, and fortified wines are the forte.

The south-east is very different. From Somerset West all the way down to Cape Agulhas, vineyards are being essayed, and the story is generally a cool or very cool one. Elgin (within Overberg) and Walker Bay are the names you are most likely to encounter, for nervy, teasing Chardonnay, sometimes coaxed towards Burgundian fullness; positively bracing Sauvignon Blanc; and some ambitious Pinot Noir, too. The ever-adaptable Shiraz is there, too, though stylistically this lean beast would be better named Syrah.

Fine wines South Africa's finest wines, both red and white, unquestionably compete at the highest levels internationally for complexity, balance, refinement and ageability. The problem facing both producers and consumers is that few yet do this consistently. Stellenbosch and Swartland are two large areas in which there are outstanding vineyards to be found, and winemaking skills using fruit sourced elsewhere are much in evidence in Franschhoek. Ambitions are laudably high in cooler-climate areas – but South Africa still lacks what other wine-producing nations have taken to calling 'icons' (wines which achieve regularly high auction or resale prices abroad).

Fun wines South Africa's fun wines include most Pinotage, most Chardonnay and most Sauvignon Blanc. The country still offers some of the best-value inexpensive white wines sold internationally. There are producers who make humour a part of their marketing (like Fairview's Charles Back), but the overall tone is often more serious here than elsewhere.

National strengths Mid-weight balance, elegance and diversity.

National weaknesses Some tough, ugly reds; some unsuccessfully austere cool-climate wines.

**PROJECT 18
PLACES:**
Portugal

Iberia's dreamy west dissolves into the Atlantic with a suite of strangely beautiful aromas and flavours. The rolling waves created a history of great fortified wines for this maritime nation; now, though, it is unfortified wines, crackling with mineral energy, which beckon drinkers. Intriguing native grape varieties, cooled geological fire and ever-changeable skies guarantee Portugal an exciting fine-wine future.

Portuguese Wines

TRY Both a traditional Baga-based Bairrada red and a Dão red (prices are often attractive), and see which you like best on its own – as well as with food.

TRY A red from the Alentejo, noticing its soft textures compared to other Portuguese red-wine classics.

TRY The best Douro red you can afford for a special occasion. Give it plenty of time, and plenty of air.

TRY A range of Portuguese whites, and expect the unexpected.

OPPOSITE ABOVE Quinta de la Rosa's terraced vineyards are typically dizzying, cut from the schist in the nineteenth century.

OPPOSITE BELOW Douro tradition may be for port, but few doubt that this will soon be one of Europe's greatest areas for table wine, too.

Wine-lovers adore Portugal. Nothing, I should warn you, is easy here; almost everything, though, is rewarding. Grape varieties? Portugal can very nearly rival Italy for extent and obscurity. Much the same goes for wine styles: Portugal has always cut its own path, no matter how perplexing that path may appear to outsiders. (Believe me, nothing is more perplexing when you drink it for the first time than red vinho verde: dark, acidic, tannic yet almost fleshless, as shocking and as disconcerting as running

naked into a hailstorm.) If all that sounds worrying, let me stress the rewards, too: strange, haunting aromas in both red and white wines combined with deep, profoundly satisfying flavours you will find nowhere else. The wines are usually underpinned with refreshing acidity levels, mineral notes and fine intrinsic balance; they age well. Portugal is a land of grandeur without excess.

The Algarve is Portugal's least distinguished wine-producing area. In the vast, sunny, savannah-like tracts of the inland Alentejo, by contrast, you'll find open, airy forests of cork oak sharing the land with cereal fields, olive groves, sheep walks – and occasional vineyards. This is the home of Portugal's softest and most affable reds, many including fruit from one of the world's rare red-fleshed grape varieties, Alicante Bouschet. Closer to Lisbon lies a patchwork of fascinating specialities, some (like sandy Colares and Estoril's Carcavelos) seemingly doomed by the encroaching city. The broad Setúbal peninsula to the south of the city, though, continues to produce its traditional

Muscat as well as a range of dry reds and whites under the Palmela name.

The plains of the Tagus, north of Lisbon, constitute Portugal's agricultural heartland, and the often light red and white wine of this area (known as the Ribatejo, the 'banks of the Tagus') is a commodity crop among many. Estremadura, on the Atlantic coast, continues the bulk theme.

Then comes excitement – with Bairrada and its neighbour Dão. Bairrada, the smaller of the two, is more susceptible to maritime moodiness: the Baga grape and rich, limey clay soils produce, in a good vintage, dark tannic reds chiselled with acidity that seem to translate Madiran or Barolo into nasal Portuguese. (Baga from Bairrada also makes much of the celebrated Mateus Rosé, many drinkers' introduction to Portuguese wine.)

Dão may lie next door, but it's a very different region: a rumpled granite upland where a wide range of Portuguese varieties produce more dark, taut reds of increasingly fruited complexity. Both Bairrada and Dão produce fine white wines, and the best of both regions have terrific ageing potential, recognized by the Portuguese tradition of *garrafeira* wines (given extended ageing, usually in both cask and bottle, before sale).

The Douro Valley, further north still, is where port is made (see next page). Recently, though, its producers have begun to use some of their finest fruit to create ambitious unfortified dry wines – and the region is being reborn. These dizzying flanks of schist, painstakingly terraced over hundreds of years, not only seem set to produce Portugal's greatest reds, but some of the world's most memorable, too. Their dimensions are as generous as anything you can find in California or Australia, though their mineral depths and bittersweet fruits make their character more challenging. The best wines of Tras-os-Montes, further north, return a lighter echo. Vinho verde, by contrast, between the mountains and the sea, growing amidst garden vegetation of almost jungle-like fecundity, is generally a tingling, light-alcohol white – though seek out that shocking red version if you visit.

WHAT PEOPLE LOVE ABOUT

Portugese Wines

+ The complexity, depth and ability to age of the traditional reds.
+ The unusual fragrances and flavours of the white wines.
+ The drama and density of the new generation of table wines from the Douro.

Port and Madeira

TRY Sercial or Verdelho Madeira as an aperitif.

TRY Vintage Madeira, at least once in your life. Nineteenth-century examples can still be located; buy from a reputable merchant to avoid fakes.

TRY Vintage port when it is first released: immature, of course, but no wine on earth tastes quite as exciting as young Vintage port.

TRY Chilled tawny port in warm summer weather.

TRY White port with ice – or mixed with tonic water.

WHAT PEOPLE LOVE ABOUT

Port and Madeira

+ The generosity, depth and exuberance of black and red fruit flavours in Vintage or Late Bottled Vintage port.
+ The smoothness and succulence of aged tawny port.
+ The vivacity, elegance and baked tang of Madeira.
+ The ability of both Vintage port and Vintage Madeira to hold the years at bay – and mark the anniversaries in a human lifetime.

OPPOSITE Quinta do Vesuvio, its very name promising tectonically exciting port of lava-like richness, is one of the region's great historic estates: remote, hot, silent, beautiful.

These two great fortified wines are the children of history. Madeira most obviously: any island sited 640 km off the African coast in a largely empty ocean was always going to seduce those under sail. It was, indeed, a long, ballasting roll down to the Caribbean, the casks packed like sardines in the belly of a ship, which created the wine we know today. Fortification prevented a vinegary decline; even more miraculously, tropical heat smoothed its spiky contours and burnished its intrinsic tang. American connoisseurs on the eastern seaboard paid high prices for wines which had crossed the Equator twice. The ships still call at Madeira, but none now needs wine as ballast – so those former journeys are duplicated in one of two ways. The best wines rest for long years in warm attics; less expensive wines spend three months in large tanks kept at the temperature of a hot July day in Riyadh – 45°C (113°F). Anonymous Madeira tends to be made from the all-purpose Tinta Negra Mole variety, but great sipping wines are based on Sercial (dry), Verdelho (medium-dry), Bual (medium-sweet) and Malmsey or Malvasia (sweet). Buy the oldest you can: age equals beauty on the Enchanted Isles. Vintage Madeira is the summit: it doesn't see the inside of a bottle until it's already 20 years old, and the best will then last a human lifetime or more. It's expensive, but a thimbleful satisfies, and you don't need to hurry to finish the bottle.

Most of the wine produced along the Douro as it squirms out of Spain and home to the Atlantic is still fortified, despite the recent success of its magnificently architectural dry table wines. Lost farms, high in the hills; an implacable summer; vines roots fumbling amid soft, foliated stone for moisture; grapes trodden into inky oblivion in granite tanks: the sweetness you taste in port is hard won. Quality is shaded more elaborately than on Madeira, though the magic word 'Vintage' still signifies the very best: thunderclap wines which need 10 years to become approachable, and which can then pass 30 or 40 in increasingly graceful serenity. 'Vintage Character', counterintuitively, is not the same thing, though it can be a jolly mouthful; 'Late Bottled Vintage', too, is a softer incarnation (though those versions labelled 'Traditional' or 'Bottle Matured' will, like true Vintage port, need decanting). Tawny port is a paler, smoother style, reaching maturity in the barrel before bottling.

The greatest ports tend to be blended, but you will find ports from single properties, too: the word to look for is *Quinta*, which means 'farm'. What about grape varieties? There were once 20 or 30 in every bottle of port; plantings are now somewhat simplified, yet even so no port is ever varietal. Touriga Nacional is universally admired; other great port grapes include Touriga Franca, Tinta Roriz (Tempranillo), Tinto Cão and Tinta Barroca. White port – glycerous, heady, almond-rich – broadens the spectrum, though it never touches the same heights.

FACT FILE: Portugal

Fine wines Great Vintage port has always been a collector's wine, and comparing different shippers' efforts with the same vintage at 20 or 30 years old a favourite wine game. Vintage Madeira is rarer, still more expensive, but unique in character – and no other wine on earth ages with such ease. Portugal's greatest red table wines, and in particular the new stars of the Douro Valley, are world class.

Fun wines Most Portuguese wine provides enormous fun for wine enthusiasts, and Portuguese rosé is great fun for wine beginners, too. Vinho verde is the white-wine equivalent of France's Beaujolais or Beaujolais-Villages: a light-hearted quaffer of singular style.

National strengths A huge diversity of wines made with a profusion of native grapes.

National weaknesses Some Portuguese wines can be puzzling or incomprehensible to outsiders, and some are overly rustic.

**PROJECT 19
PLACES:
Germany**

Germany? Time to retune the radio. Everything is different here. To enjoy great German wine to the full, you need to forget you have ever drunk wine before. Then, into the silence of your expectation, comes a wine music conjured from rain-washed air, dappled valleys and breezy orchards: nature's fruits, sketched with gossamer restraint. Great slopes of slate and limestone add mineral gravity.

The Mosel Valley

TRY Riesling from the Saar, and compare it to Riesling from the Pfalz: you'll find a world of difference.

TRY Look out for Germany's Trocken wines: they are hugely improved on those of the past. Have the techniques been mastered – or is it global warming in action?

TRY A Spätburgunder from Assmannshausen or Baden, and compare it with a red Burgundy of the same price: you may be surprised by your preference.

TRY There's more to Germany than Riesling: look out for exciting Scheurebe, Muskateller, even Viognier.

The River Mosel has its roots in France and Luxembourg; it drains Belgian fields, too. It enters Germany near Trier, and from here to Koblenz it slides its way, with glassy imperturbility, past vast slopes, walls and ramps of slate, some of them soaring 200 metres or more into the air. As past millennia ticked by, the rock forced the water to cut dozens of curves and make at least eight giant horseshoe turns. It's only thanks to the play of water, stone and light along the length of this stately slalom that vines have any function at all this far north. That role is unique. White grapes here (the best always Riesling) tiptoe towards a delicate, virginal maturity. They stop fermenting with no more alcohol in them than in a glass of Trappist beer. They capture fruit flavours, though, with photographic limpidity and fidelity. Sugar and acidity are locked into a perfectly weighted embrace inside them, like cogs in a watch. A taste of wine should always be a taste of the natural world, but a glass of Mosel Riesling doesn't merely evoke the vivid orchard fruits of a northern autumn; it

actually seems to comprise the essence of those fruits, with the memory of slate adding extra dignity and profundity. The Mosel's two tributaries, the Saar and the Ruwer, lift that delicacy to a still higher pitch.

The drinker's choice is generally to buy drier or sweeter versions, coming from more or less celebrated vineyards. How do you tell which is which? Complications abound, but *trocken* (dry) and *halbtrocken* (medium-dry) are the key words denoting the drier end of the spectrum; QbA and QmP Kabinett wines shouldn't be overly sweet, either. My favourite is Kabinett: perfect refreshment. Spätlese, Auslese, Eiswein, Beerenauslese and Trockenbeerenauslese progressively swell the sweet notes. Great vineyards are best diagnosed, alas, by high price. (And vice versa: cheap Mosel is a sugary disappointment.) If you want to look out for just three great Mosel vineyards, remember the sundial from Wehlen (Wehlener Sonnenuhr), the spice garden from Ürzig (Ürziger Würzgarten) and the doctor from Bernkastel (Bernkasteler Doctor).

The Rhine Valley

For most of its German existence, the Rhine flows north. Since winegrowing in Germany means finding a sunny, sheltered slope, a gigantic river eddying north is little use. With one exception, then, the great vineyards of the Rhine are created by the many tributaries which flow into it (the most famous of which is the Mosel) and the sunny, south-facing side valleys they create.

That one exception is called the Rheingau. Between Mainz and Bingen the river flows from east to west, and some of Germany's lordliest Rieslings come into being in the sonorously named vineyards which stretch back from its northern bank. The wines are bigger in frame than those of the Mosel, Saar and Ruwer, though their balance can be no less electric. As the river turns north again, Pinot Noir-based red wines of surprising depth become a brief speciality, at Assmannshausen. The scenery along what is called the Mittelrhein, north to Bonn, is even grander and more Wagnerian, though side valleys are now in shorter supply.

Three wine regions crowd the Rhine to the south of Mainz. The first is Rheinhessen on the river's south and west banks: once an easy-going Liebfraumilch factory, but increasingly a chance for the keen to prove that rolling green hills can produce wine to rival that of soaring slate slopes. The second is the Pfalz: warm enough to ripen almonds and grow tobacco, giving Rieslings of plump, spicy deliciousness in which mineral notes take second place to an intoxication of fruit. And the third is Baden: Alsace's German twin, and the home of Germany's most emphatic food wines, both red and white. Most are dry; many are strong.

In each of these regions, Riesling's Teutonic pre-eminence is challenged by other varieties: chewy Silvaner and Weissburgunder (Pinot Blanc); the intensely aromatic Scheurebe and Muskateller; spicy Grauburgunder (Pinot Gris, often called Ruländer when made in a sweeter style); and lively reds based on Dornfelder and Spätburgunder (Pinot Noir).

WHAT PEOPLE LOVE ABOUT

Mosel Wines

+ Their exquisite delicacy and balance.
+ Their ability to evoke, with astonishing sensual fidelity, nature's flowers and fruits.
+ Their low alcohol levels.
+ The improbable ease with which the best age.

Rhine Wines

+ The rarely cloying richness of their traditionally made wines.
+ The balance and depth of their dry wines.
+ Their perfume and wealth of flavour.
+ Their new-found diversity in terms of both style and grape variety.

ABOVE Autumn in the Rheingau, where a gentle end of season is a regular gift to growers. Riesling leaves turn briefly golden before the first frosts end their lives.

Other Valleys

TRY Seek out Riesling from some of the Nahe's finest sites and top growers: value is often keen compared to the Rheingau.

TRY A dry Silvaner from Franken, and compare it if you can with a Sylvaner from Alsace. The grape may no longer be a fashionable one, but these richly dry wines can be excellent, especially with food.

TRY A Riesling from Franken – to see Germany's greatest grape in unusual guise.

WHAT PEOPLE LOVE ABOUT

Franken Wines

+ Their chewy dryness.
+ Their vivid, exciting but always ripe acid balance.
+ Their food-friendliness.
+ Their unusual bottles.

The River Nahe, like the Mosel itself, is a westerly tributary of the Rhine, joining the river at Bingen. It's smaller than the Mosel, a compilation of streams trickling from the Hunsrück and Saarland hills, yet its glittering variety of soils, slopes and sites provides an inspiring canvas for ambitious growers. For great wines, we are still in the kingdom of Riesling, especially when those wines are grown in the steep, mineral-rich quartzite and slate slopes to the south-west of Bad Kreuznach. Nahe's finest contrive to be pungent, crisp and delicate by turn, providing subtly nuanced echoes of both the Mosel and the Rheingau. By dint of northerliness?

Not necessarily. Nothing in German wine is quite as unexpected as the fact that the Ahr Valley, much further north and within easy touring reach of Bonn and Köln, specializes in Spätburgunder-based red wines on its steep, south-facing slate slopes. Despite their latitude, a warm summer and a hard-pruning grower can conjure pungent and vivacious Pinot Noir from the dark stone.

The Ahr was, prior to German unification, a northerly outpost; now it is surpassed by Saale-Unstrut and Sachsen, both well on the way to Poland and the latter on Dresden's doorstep. Summer warmth, when it finally sets in and supposing that frost hasn't scratched the buds into oblivion first, is enough to hurry a handful of varieties towards ripeness here on favoured southern slopes. Those following the Bach trail, or pursuing Meissen shepherdesses, are duly grateful. Tiny Hessische Bergstrasse

is a morsel of Baden stranded in the neighbouring state of Hessen. The wines of Württemberg, like those of Saale-Unstrut and Sachsen, principally slake local thirsts – in this case, those of Stuttgart. Light red and soft white by the tumblerful is the local way. Trollinger (the same grape as the Schiava of Italy's Alto Adige) is the stodgy star, but Riesling, the oddly named Schwarzriesling (in fact Champagne's Pinot Meunier) and darker Lemberger are important, too.

The greatest German wine region aside from those which cluster along the Rhine is unquestionably Franken. Forget filigree delicacy; forget orchard fruits and hedgerow flowers; forget slate. Franken's greatest wines are forcefully dry Silvaner and Riesling whites grown on stately limestone hillsides to the east of sumptuous, baroque Würzburg. Their electric force and balance may still be distinctively German, but in other ways they almost provide a northern echo of France's ever-popular Chablis. Aromatic varieties like Kerner, Bacchus and Scheurebe perform well here; so, too, do red Spätburgunder and Frühburgunder (another clone of Pinot Noir) on sandstone slopes to the west of Würzberg. Franken's flask-like bottles are amusingly unmistakable, apparently modelled on the nether regions of a billy goat. Or are they teasing?

OPPOSITE Schloss Johannisberg in all its winter grandeur. The vines are almost snug in the snow. The new wines in the cellars, meanwhile, throw crystals of tartar when the temperature drops.

FACT FILE: Germany

Fine wines Some wine lovers are convinced that German Riesling is the world's greatest white wine, by virtue of its exquisite clarity and definition, its balance, its freshness, its mineral charge and its seemingly effortless ability to age. It is, though, so different in style from the international norm that other drinkers find this accolade puzzling. Germany's finest wines are of Kabinett quality or better, from the distinguished growers of the Mosel, Saar, Ruwer, Nahe, Rheingau and Pfalz, in great vintages. Other regions and other grapes offer increasingly close competition.

Fun wines Forget turgid national stereotypes; there is lots of fun built into German wine, from the milky, half-fermented new wine sold each autumn in the wine regions, via entertainingly aromatic varieties such as Bacchus and Scheurebe, to entire regions (like Baden and Württemberg) which refuse to take themselves or their wines too seriously.

National strengths A grand wine tradition of unmatched singularity and refinement.

National weaknesses Confusingly complicated wine law, and cheap wines which tarnish the country's image.

**PROJECT 20
PLACES:
Other Countries**

The journey is almost over, but in another sense it is just beginning: ceaseless change characterizes the wine world just as it does existence itself. The countries I describe over the next eight pages already produce great though little-known wines; in future years, as global warming melts our settled assumptions, we may come to see many of them in a new light. Winegrowing is always work in progress.

Austria

TRY A Grüner Veltliner with food. More fun than a southern-hemisphere Chardonnay of the same price?

TRY A sweet wine from the Burgenland: they can be astonishingly good value.

TRY The best Austrian Riesling you can find – and, if possible, compare it with an Alsace Grand Cru.

WHAT PEOPLE LOVE ABOUT

Austrian Wines
+ Their dryness.
+ Their depth and concentration.
+ The Heurige (heady new wine) served in Viennese taverns in autumn.
+ The pliant character of Grüner Veltliner.

Austria's mountainous west is a land of conifers and ski-runs rather than vines and cellars. Its lower-lying east, by contrast, is rich in vineyards. Names and bottles may put you in mind of Germany. The analogy, today, is falser than ever. Austria is unique: a land of dry, heady whites full of pepper, fire, stone and fruit. Some outflank white burgundy as meals-in-a-glass; others outperform Alsace as divas of scented excess. Reds can acquire the structure of true southerners. In Burgenland, where the shallow, marsh-fringed Neusiedlersee brings botrytis as regularly as December brings Christmas, some of Europe's most succulently sweet wines ooze into being. When you reach Austria, expect the unexpected.

Austria's noblest wines are found along the banks of the Danube (Donau) in the Wachau, Kremstal and Kamptal, west of Vienna. Hot, lazy summer days, billowing up the serpentine river from Hungary's Pannonian plain, bring extravagant ripeness. After nightfall, cool air slides down from the steep woodlands above, maintaining acidity levels. Austria has a grape to call its own, and the Grüner Veltliner (occupying over a third of the country's vineyards) makes supremely refreshing dry wine, sometimes light and spritzy but, when made with more ambition, chewy and hauntingly scented, an agreeably understated melange of pith and plant. (It's a superb partner for Asian food, by the way.) Riesling, especially on the best slopes of the Wachau, memorably combines force with allusiveness. Chardonnay (sometimes called Morillon) is startlingly credible in Austria, and Weissburgunder (Pinot Blanc), Traminer and even the old workhorse Müller-Thurgau can put on an impressive turn of speed when yields are kept low. Red wines, once confined to a few areas, are now widely harvested: Zweigelt, Blauer Portugieser, Blaufränkisch (Limberger or Lemberger) and St Laurent are all names unfamiliar to non-Austrians, but Pinot Noir (locally known as Blauburgunder) and even Cabernet Sauvignon show up on labels, too. Oak is often used with enthusiasm.

Switzerland

The most dazzling proof of European devotion to wine is found not in Bordeaux, or Tuscany, or the Rhine. It's found here, in Switzerland, the land of milk and muesli. Nowhere else does quite as much effort go into growing a few vines – on a fillet of scree between lake and motorway, on a sunny morsel of hillside, on a scrap of sheltered mountain accessible only by foot. Toy funicular railways and cable sleighs exist to transport grapes alone. Sensible banking careers underwrite weekends of vineyard hard labour. Yet everyone feels it's worth it: 98 out of every 100 bottles of Swiss wine are drunk in Switzerland. Expensively.

Switzerland's wines, typically enough for a mountainous land where every valley would once have been a country to itself, are hugely diverse. Its salty-buttery Chasselas (sometimes called Fendant) is a world original; smooth Gamay gets plenty of Swiss glasstime; Pinot Noir fuels dreams of grandeur, and occasionally sees them realized; Merlot, in Italian-speaking Ticino, can compete with Bolgheri. Just.

The biggest wine-producing canton is Valais: these are, in fact, the first vineyards of the Rhône Valley, long before the river snakes into France. Valais is one of the rare places where you can taste wine made from the fecund mother of Chardonnay, Aligoté, Gamay and Melon: Gouais Blanc, here called Gwäss. It almost merits a pilgrimage. The red Dôle is usually a Gamay-Pinot Noir blend; Syrah, today, is increasingly common. Indigenous grapes include white Petite Arvine, Amigne and Païen, also called Heida; reds include Cornalin and Humagne Rouge.

Next in importance after Valais comes Vaud: most of its vineyards lie on south-facing slopes on the north bank of Lake Geneva, where they can sip its reflected sunshine. Chasselas is most at home here, at its best in the villages of Calamin and Dézaley. Geneva itself has seen a flurry of innovation in recent years, with the default option of Chasselas often now surrendering to Gamay and Pinot Noir. Even Sauvignon Blanc and Merlot have been making their way to the populous lake's end.

TRY A good Swiss Chasselas: salty-fresh, yet surprisingly rich and full-flavoured, too.

TRY A Swiss Pinot, and compare it with one of the lighter 'village' wines from Burgundy, like Santenay, St Romain or Monthelie.

WHAT PEOPLE LOVE ABOUT

Swiss Wines
+ The fact that they exist at all.
+ The light, refreshing qualities of Swiss red wines.
+ The huge spectrum of aromas, flavours and alcohol levels in Swiss white wines.
+ Switzerland's extraordinary range of indigenous and historical varieties.

ABOVE Not a scene you'd readily associate with the Rhône Valley – but here the river is, in its Swiss infancy, stealing through vineyards filled with ancient, half-forgotten varieties.

Greece

TRY A dry white from Santorini, based on Assyrtiko, either as an aperitif or with fish or seafood, and compare it to Chablis.

TRY A red Naoussa, and compare it to a Barbaresco or Nebbiolo (Spanna) from Piedmont.

TRY Keep an open mind about retsina. Don't serve it too cold, and try it with Greek food.

WHAT PEOPLE LOVE ABOUT

Greek Wines

+ The perfume and purity of the best Greek whites.
+ The intrinsic class and complexity of the best Greek reds.
+ Greece's ancient grape varieties and wine traditions including retsina, Santorini's Vinsanto, Samos' Nectar and Mavrodaphne of Patras.

Greece, strange to say, has much in common with Switzerland. Both countries are devoted to wine; and both lands are mountainous, that rugged surface preserving ancient varieties and specialities in inaccessible corners far longer than those living in easier terrains would have managed. Swiss vines tend to gaze on rivers and lakes; Greek vines often bask in the glitter of sunlight on the Aegean.

Wine is made everywhere in Greece. Everywhere accessible, that is. International varietals may be infiltrating the country's vineyards, soaking up buoyant domestic demand; yet it is Greece's own grape varieties which best reward the curious drinker. Two are world-class: the red Xinomavro, as grown across northern Greece but especially in Naoussa and Goumenissa, providing craggy, authoritative wines with fine ageing potential; and the white Assyrtiko which, when rooted in the pumice and ash of the volcanic island of Santorini, provides one of the most mineral of all whites, and one whose bright, diving

acidity never ceases to shock. Red Agiorgitiko flourishes in Nemea on the Peleponnese, making an easier, softer-textured red than Xinomavro can manage. Sweet white Muscat (especially on Samos) and red Mavrodaphne (from Patras) comfort. Other Greek grape varieties worth pouncing on (if you can fathom the labels) include the white Malagousia, Athiri, Roditis and Moschofilero and the red Mandilaria. In addition to the regions above, Amindeo is a fascinating, cool-climate location producing impressive wines from a range of varieties.

And retsina? It's a beautiful and poetic combination of white wine made from Attica's Saviatano and flavoured with less than 1% of resin, tapped from the trunks of Aleppo pines (*Pinus halepensis*). It's best drunk from tumblers, within sight and sigh of the sea.

ABOVE Santorini's ash and pumice soils are some of the wine world's youngest. These Assyrtiko vines make a dry white of compelling mineral beauty from them.

Bulgaria and Slovenia

Bulgaria, at the dawn of the twenty-first century, was a fallen star. It had been awesomely successful at producing easy-going, tasty varietal wines during the decade prior to communism's collapse in 1989. That collapse led to viticultural catastrophe, as former collective farms were given back, tiny parcel by tiny parcel, to the scattered descendants of those who owned the land in 1947. The recovery is now in place, but it will take time. The stakes are high, though: Bulgaria has the potential to be a kind of European Chile, producing soft, amenable, round-contoured reds and lively, articulate whites with little difficulty.

All of France's key varieties flourish here, most notably Cabernet Sauvignon, Merlot and Chardonnay; Bulgaria's own red Mavrud and Melnik varieties, and the white Dimiat and Rkatsiteli, have much to offer. The three main producing regions (all large, with a variety of climates and soils) are Bulgaria's Danubian Plain in the north (for lively reds), the Black Sea coast (where whites predominate), and the vast Thracian

Lowlands, which lie between the central Stara Planina Mountains and southern Rhodope Mountains, where red wines can acquire flesh, structure and depth. Thrace, the Bulgarians love to point out, was the mythical home of both Dionysus and Orpheus.

Slovenia, wedged between Austria to its north and Italy's Friuli to its west, grasped independence with both hands in 1992, and its winemakers have subsequently competed enthusiastically with their Austrian and Italian neighbours. White wines predominate, many of the most interesting among them made from the local Ribolla Gialla grape variety, but fresh reds are increasingly impressive, too. Oak is sometimes used over-exuberantly; look out, in the long run, for perfumed freshness and a crisp flavour focus.

ABOVE Bulgaria's transition to wine-producing modernity has been hesitant, but few European countries can make such a good job of producing tasty, well-rounded reds. The best is yet to come.

TRY Some of Bulgaria's new-wave red wines made from reconstituted and replanted vineyards, often with overseas investment help, to understand the country's potential.

TRY A Slovenian white made from Ribolla Gialla – and compare it with a Slovenian Chardonnay or Sauvignon Blanc. Which do you prefer?

WHAT PEOPLE LOVE ABOUT

Bulgarian Wines

+ Their simple varietal labelling and lack of confusing regional names.
+ The soft, supple, ripe style and clear varietal character of Bulgarian red wines from the communist heyday – now slowly returning with outside investment help.

Slovenian Wines

+ A freshness and crisp profile in both white and red wines – and attractive value for money compared to Friulian or Austrian competition.

Hungary and Tokaji

TRY The most expensive Hungarian white wine based on an indigenous grape variety that you can find: the differential with cheap wines based on international varieties is likely to be stark.

TRY A 5-puttonyos Aszú Tokaji. Drink it on its own, and give it plenty of time to open and blossom in the glass.

WHAT PEOPLE LOVE ABOUT

Hungarian Wines

+ The firm, rich, chewy quality of traditional Hungarian white wines.
+ The lively depths of new-wave Hungarian reds.
+ The complexity, balance and unique stye of Tokaji.

ABOVE LEFT Eastern Europe's greatest wine, in the twenty-first century as in the eighteenth, is vivacious, burnished Tokaji.

ABOVE RIGHT A little house in the vineyards: every Tokaji farmer's dream. That scrub could be fine vineyard too, by the way.

Hungary's history has left it with a distinguished and complex wine tradition which the twentieth century's years of war and dilapidation failed to obliterate. It's gradually returning to life, like a faded fresco in restoration. Red wines thrive in the far south, especially in Villány, where Cabernet and Merlot can ripen vivaciously; those of the Mátra Hills to the north-west of Budapest are generally lighter, fish-friendly reds.

It is with white wines, though, that Hungary excels, especially those based on its two greatest domestic varieties, Furmint and Hárslevelü. Furmint is the less aromatic, but its masterful, insistent, sappy strength and flavour can make an astonishingly good food wine; Hárslevelü (its Hungarian name evoking the linden tree, which perfumes high summer across central Europe) is softer and more fragrant. International varieties are much planted, too – look out for Pinot Gris (locally called Szürzkebarát), which comes into its own on the shores of Lake Balaton.

The volcanic-soiled and loess-blown hills of Tokaji, in the far north-east of the county,

mother Hungary's greatest vineyards. The principal grape varieties are Furmint and Hárslevelü, but it is a wine of method as much as of variety. That method involves picking healthy and rotten (botrytis-affected) grapes separately. Dry wines are made with the former, into which varying amounts of a sweet paste formed of the latter are tipped prior to fermentation or refermentation (the choice is the grower's). Then it's off into cold, mould-filled cellars to age, sometimes with a headspace in the cask. The result is a spectrum of wines from dry (Szamorodni Száraz) to sweet (Aszú), with the sweetness measured in 'hods' or *puttonyos*. (Eszencia, a fragrant syrup, is the barely fermented seepings from the botrytized berries.) Sugar isn't the point, though: great Tokaji is the taste of autumn. The orchard sweetness of apricot and peach is somehow rendered as a memory in Tokaji, qualified by the acid tang of experience. There are leafy notes and forest airs, especially as time passes; there is the savoury undertow we haltingly call umami. It is complete as few wines are.

Lebanon, Israel and North Africa

Anyone familiar with the books of the Bible will need no reminding of the ancient importance of winegrowing in the eastern Mediterranean. This is the land where burdensome bunches of grapes grew by the brook of Eschol, of the miracle at Cana, of a last supper whose anonymous wine is evoked many millions of times every year.

Lebanon and Israel are, today, overly hot for fine winegrowing – at sea level. Climb 1,000 metres up, though, as you can do in the Bekaa Valley and on the Israeli-occupied Golan Heights, and the equation changes. Winters can be cold, even snowy; summer nights are cool. Both locations can produce outstandingly soft, savoury yet poised red wines and impressively fresh whites, generally based on international grape varieties – though whether those of Bordeaux or those of the southern Rhône and Languedoc will prove most suitable to these sites in the long run is still an open question. (As, of course, is the issue of whether the Golan Heights will remain Israeli territory. New plantings have concentrated on less disputed though still-cool Galilee vineyards close to the Lebanese border.)

The three countries of western North Africa (Tunisia, Algeria and Morocco) enjoyed, by the mid-twentieth century, two-thirds of the international wine trade. This figure seems barely credible now. It was the creation of French colonial power; it dissipated after independence.

Daybreak, from Tunis to Marrakech, begins with the echoing beauty of the muezzin's call to prayer. There is, consequently, little domestic interest in wine, and a tenuous base on which to build – despite frequently highly propitious growing conditions and still extensive vineyards full of often old vines. Tunisian Muscat and red Mornag; Algerian Tlemcen; and Moroccan Beni M'Tir, Guerrouane and Coteaux d'Atlas are all occasionally noteworthy survivors. Recent French investors (including Bordeaux's Bernard Magrez, working with wine-loving actor Gérard Depardieu) are now rekindling the embers.

TRY Merlot from the Golan Heights and red blends from the Bekaa Valley – and compare.

TRY Look out for the vin gris (literally 'grey wine' – a traditional if downbeat way of referring to pale rosé in North Africa) from Morocco's Boulaouane or Tunisia's Tébourba.

WHAT PEOPLE LOVE ABOUT

Lebanese Wines

+ The heroism of their continued production throughout Lebanon's civil war and recent Israeli invasions.
+ The soft, gentle flavour spectrum of its red wines – and their gratifying ability to modulate with time.

ABOVE At 1,000 metres and shielded from the Mediterranean by Mount Lebanon, Bekaa Valley winters can be cold enough for a blanket of snow. These dormant vines belong to Château Kefraya.

Romania and Moldova

TRY Romania's soft way with both Pinot Noir and Merlot, especially from the Dealu Mare region.

TRY A Moldovan Pinot Gris, and compare it to other versions from Alsace and from New Zealand. Which offers best value?

WHAT PEOPLE LOVE ABOUT

Romanian and Moldovan Wines

+ Their value for money.
+ The approachable and easy-drinking international varietals.
+ Their specialities and traditions – even if these are hard to find at present.

ABOVE Transylvania is one of Romania's cooler areas, and the source of some of its freshest white wines. These Tirnave vineyards and their artless hayricks emphasize the spaciousness of Eastern Europe's second-largest country.

Romania, like Bulgaria to its south, is a sleeping wine giant. Like Hungary, its wine traditions are long and intricate. Like France, Italy, Spain and Portugal, its people speak a Romance language rather than a Slavic one; like those nations, too, its people love to uncork a bottle of wine rather than toss back vodka or sip brandy at dinner. Its wine-producing potential is exciting, even if substantially unrealized at present.

The Carpathian Mountains form a boomerang which arcs through the centre of the country. Most of Romania's wine comes into being to the east, in gently undulating Romanian Moldova (the rich white Cotnari is a time-honoured speciality), and to the south, where the Carpathian foothills provide a long chain of outstanding south-facing slopes (look out for a range of reds from Dealu Mare and the increasingly impressive Drăgăşani and Sâmbureşti regions). The warm, sunny Black Sea coast is a source of full-bodied reds as well as sweet, late-harvest Chardonnay (Murfatlar is a key name). High, cool Transylvania provides

the country's crispest whites, and there are more light reds up on the Hungarian border (Banat). Familiar varietals answer present international demand, but let's hope the great Romanian varieties (like the white Fetească Albă, Grasă and Tămâioasă Românească and the red Fetească Neagră) travel further in future. If they are to have the success they deserve, though, then consumers all over the world must be prepared to buy wine made from a grape whose name very few of them can pronounce, coming from a country whose existing reputation is almost exclusively for cheap wine. Are we drinkers ready to rise to the challenge?

Independent Moldova, to Romania's east, is vine-swathed, thanks to its former role as cellarer to the USSR. Survival has been difficult and prosperity is still a dream, but the country's best wines (mainly international varietals, including some outstanding Pinot Gris) are satisfying, well-made and substantial. Look out, too, for dark reds from Purcari.

Georgia, Armenia, Ukraine, Russia, England and Wales

Ours is a strange world. Nothing could be easier than drinking wine from Tasmania and Patagonia, yet finding internationally competitive bottles from the birthplace of wine itself, modern Georgia and Armenia, is a challenge. These two countries, Georgia in particular, have fine indigenous varieties – and winemaking traditions, too, of awesome antiquity (the Georgian *marani* is an outdoor cellar, its vats earthenware vessels buried to their very rims in the earth). Look out, chance permitting, for red Georgian Saperavi and Armenian Areni. Ukraine's Crimea (Krym) is where the Russian imperial winemaking legacy lives on at Massandra: dessert wines are the historical greats, but there is a substantial sparkling wine tradition, too. Russia's own vineyards are concentrated near the coasts of three seas: Black, Azov and Caspian. The country's wealthiest and most ambitious estate owners will eventually challenge preconceptions based on the rough, sweet wines of Soviet days.

England's winegrowers (and a smaller Welsh contingent) have already provided surprises. Early efforts in England were based on German varieties and German styles; haphazard winemaking from hobby-winegrowers gave the wines a reputation for unreliability. Today's winegrowers are more professional; and the fact that both Chardonnay and Pinot Noir can now be coaxed into the austere ripeness which provides great sparkling base wine is providing an excuse for Champagne's elite to come and take a look at the south-facing chalk slopes of Kent, Sussex, Surrey and Hampshire, and warmer sites in the West Country. Provided the vital storage period following the second fermentation isn't rushed, then English sparkling wines can indeed compete on equal terms with much Champagne. Look out, in addition to sparkling wine, for slenderly dry whites of great aromatic charm, often still based on recherché German crossings, and even some plausible Pinot, too.

WHAT PEOPLE LOVE ABOUT

English Wines

+ The depth, rigour and complexity of the best English sparkling wines.
+ Light and lively dry white wines with subtle hedgerow fragrance.
+ Pale Pinot without too much alcohol – but with balanced and lively flavours of true varietal fidelity.

ABOVE The vines of sparkling wine pioneer Nyetimber in Sussex lie within sight of the South Downs. Champagne varieties and slow maturation produce great fizz.

Glossary

abv alcohol by volume: the percentage of alcohol in a wine

acetaldehyde organic chemical compound present in plant material and fermented products, its aromatic trace most palpable in the aroma of fino sherry and manzanilla

acidification the adding of acid to wine to give it a brighter, sharper flavour

acidity a vital component of all wine, and a key structuring element in wine's flavour profile. Learning how to analyse a wine's acidity is a vital tasting skill

amontillado sherry style originally referring to an old fino on which the *flor* has expired and which is now ageing oxidatively. Also used to describe a blended sherry of medium colour, often semi-sweet or sweet

AOC *appellation d'origine contrôlée*: French term meaning 'name of controlled origin'. Appears on the labels of wines from geographically defined French wine regions; usually implies certain grape varieties, too

appellation a geographically defined wine name

barrel fermentation carrying out fermentation inside a barrel (easy for white wines; very hard but possible for red wines), to promote the smooth integration of oak flavours

blanc de blancs French term meaning 'white of whites': a white wine, usually sparkling, made from white grapes only

blanc de noirs French term meaning 'white of blacks': a white wine, usually sparkling, made from black grapes only

blind tasting tasting wine without knowing what it is: a key part of the learning process

botrytis *Botrytis cinerea* or 'noble rot': a mould attacking ripe grapes, shrivelling them and thus reducing the percentage of water they contain, as well as adding a faintly bitter-edged flavour. Harvesting botrytized

grapes is one of the two fundamental ways of making unfortified sweet wines

brut the most usual level of sweetening for sparkling wine and Champagne: 6–15 g/l

chaptalization adding sugar to must to increase final alcohol context. Also called enrichment

claret traditional British term for red Bordeaux

classé French term meaning 'classed' and signifying a particular property's inclusion in a local quality classification scheme

corked wine a wine is said to be 'corked' if it shows characteristics associated with contamination by 2,4,6-trichloroanisole: a musty, cardboardy or chemical aroma and flavour. The source is usually spoiled cork

cru French word meaning 'growth': a vineyard site and the wine made from it

demi-sec 'half-sweet' (French)

DO *denominación de origen*: Spain's equivalent of France's AOC

DOC *denominazione di origine controllata* or *denominação de origem controlada*. Italy's and Portugal's equivalent of France's AOC

DOCa *denominación de origen calificada*. Spain's equivalent of Italy's DOCG

DOCG *denominazione de origine controllata e garantita*. An Italian term supposedly 'guaranteeing' the quality of a DOC

doux 'sweet' (French)

dry farming the growing of vines without recourse to irrigation

enrichment *see* chaptalization

enzymes proteins which induce or speed biochemical change; found in grapes, yeast and must, and used as winemaking additives

extra brut term used to describe unsweetened sparkling wine or Champagne

extract the non-volatile solids in a wine, some of which will become sediment, and all of which contribute to flavour or texture

fermentation the conversion of sugar by yeast into equal quantities of alcohol and carbon dioxide

filtered most wines are filtered before bottling by passage through a membrane of varying pore size

fined a wine which has been fined is one which has had an agent added to it (called a fining) to aid its clarification

fortification the addition of high-strength alcohol to must or part-fermented wine in order to prevent or arrest fermentation, thereby retaining natural grape sugars in the finished wine. Some fully fermented dry wines (such as sherry) are also fortified in order to stabilize them prior to ageing

fruit fruit-like characters are typical of most young wines, and are a sought-after character in most inexpensive wines

grand cru 'great growth': a French term for a distinguished vineyard site and the wine made from it. The top tier of Burgundian vineyard classification

glycerol minor by-product of fermentation, with an oily texture and faintly sweet flavour, present in all wines but at high levels in sweet wines

halbtrocken 'half-sweet' (German)

hock British term for white Rhine wine

icewine sweet wine made from frozen grapes

IGT *indicazione geografica tipica*. Italy's equivalent of France's *vin de pays*, though increasingly used as an alternative to DOC

lactic milky

late harvest mature grapes are sometimes left for extended periods on the vines in order to concentrate their sugars, usually to make a sweet wine

lees the deposit left after the fermentation of wine or during the ageing process of wine. Extended contact with these deposits can bring flavour and texture to wines

maceration the soaking of must or wine with grape skins. Most common for red wines during and after fermentation, but also used for wines of both colours prior to fermentation to intensify fragrance and fruit character

malolactic fermentation, **malo** or **mlf** a bacteriological conversion of malic (sharp, appley) acid to lactic (soft, milky) acid. Undergone after alcoholic fermentation by all red wines and some white wines

Meritage Californian term to describe varietal blends imitative of Bordeaux (Cabernet Sauvignon, Merlot, Cabernet Franc, Malbec and Petit Verdot for reds; Sémillon, Sauvignon Blanc and Muscadelle for whites)

micro-oxygenation the dribbling of small amounts of oxygen through the wine to oxygenate it without racking it off its lees

monoterpenes organic compounds responsible for much of the aroma and flavour profile of wines based on Muscat, Riesling and other aromatic white varieties

must grape juice

noble rot *see* botrytis

oak trees belonging to the *Quercus* family are the primary source of wood to make barrels, tuns and vats. Oak is also used to flavour inexpensive wines via the maceration of staves or chips in the wine

oaked wine made in contact with a form of new or young oak, showing characteristics associated with oak-ageing (such as vanillic or toasty scents and flavours)

oenologist winemaker

oxidation the effect produced on a wine by extended contact with air. Beneficial and desired in some regions for some wines, most notably sherries, but generally avoided in order to maintain freshness, fruitiness and shapeliness in wine

oxygenation all wines require a little air exposure. This is achieved by oxygenation – often racking or micro-oxygenation

passerillage *see* raising

premier cru 'first growth': French term for a distinguished vineyard site and the wine made from it. The second tier of Burgundian vineyard classification, but the top tier in Bordeaux's Médoc region

racking moving wine from one vessel to another to aerate it and remove it from lees

raising allowing grapes to shrivel on the vine before picking. One of two fundamental ways of making unfortified sweet wines

reduced wines (especially young red wines) are said to be reduced or suffering from reduction when they exhibit stinky characteristics typical of sulphur compounds. Decanting such wines to oxygenate them may lessen these characteristics

sec a French term meaning 'dry' for still wines, although any sparkling wine described as 'sec' is in fact quite sweet (17–35 g/l sugar)

sediment a deposit thrown by certain wines, particularly those rich in phenolics (reactive compounds such as tannins) or those which have not been subjected to fining and filtering before bottling

séléction des grains nobles 'selection of grapes affected by noble rot', implying (in Alsace) a sweet wine

structure a wine's structure can be both tasted and felt in the mouth. Its component parts are formed by alcohol, extract, acidity, tannins and glycerol

sulphites sulphur dioxide is used to promote hygiene in winemaking, and is also a natural by-product of fermentation. Wine labels in many countries state 'contains sulphites' if the level of sulphur dioxide is over 10 mg/l,

as it usually is and as it always has been

tannins substances found in grape skins (and, to a lesser extent, wooden barrels) responsible for much of the textural dimension of wine. Analysing tannin in wine is a vital tasting skill

terroir 'placeness': French term signifying the way in which the place where a wine is made marks its character (via soil, climate, topography and local winegrowing and winemaking traditions). Enthusiasts for such traits are sometimes termed 'terroiristes'

trocken 'dry' (German)

umami the fifth primary taste, with salt, sour, sweet and bitter. This savoury characteristic is typical of some sherries and Tokaji

unoaked wine made without contact with oak

vanillins characteristic aroma and flavour derived from oak, especially white (American) oak

vendange tardive 'late harvest': French term implying some sweetness in a wine

vieilles vignes 'old vines'. Old vines are thought to produce superior wine, thanks to their low yields and deep root network

vinosity a sinewy, 'winey' character typical of many classic European white wines

vin de pays 'country wine': French classification, originally describing wines made outside AOC areas, but increasingly used to describe varietal wines made both outside and inside AOC areas

vintage a harvest, and by extension the wine of any single year. In the port-making Douro Valley, on Madeira and in Champagne, by contrast, a Vintage is an outstanding wine made from the harvest of a single great year, and intended to be kept until mature. Only the best years are 'declared' as a Vintage where blended wine is the norm

viticulture vine-growing

Index

Note: Page numbers in italics refer to captions.

Picture credits

Key: **a**=above, **b**=below, **r**=right, **l**=left, **c**=centre, **ph**=photographer.

All photographs by William Lingwood unless otherwise stated.

6 ph Alan Williams; **7 all ph** Alan Williams; **9 ph** Alan Williams; **22 ph** Alan Williams; **23 a l** © Eddie Gerald/Alamy; **23 a r ph** Alan Williams; **24 a l ph** Alan Williams/Monte Bello, Ridge Vineyards, Santa Cruz Mountains, California; **24 a c ph** Alan Williams/Maison M. Chapoutier, Tain l'Hermitage, France; **24 a r ph** Alan Williams; **24 b ph** Alan Williams/Châteauneuf du Pape, France; **28 ph** Dan Duchars/a wine cellar in a house in Surrey designed by Spiral Cellars Ltd; **30 ph** Alan Williams; **33 ph** Alan Williams; **34 ph** Alan Williams/Jordan Vineyard and Winery of Sonoma County, California; **50–59 background ph** Alan Williams; **60** © Villa Maria Estate Ltd/image courtesy of New Zealand Winegrowers; **61 ph** Alan Williams/Viña Concha y Toro, Maipo Valley, Chile; **62 a** © Villa Maria Estate Ltd/image courtesy of New Zealand Winegrowers; **62 b ph** Alan Williams; **63** © Cephas/Mick Rock; **64** © Cephas/Mick Rock; **66–71 ph** Alan Williams; **72 ph** Alan Williams/Jordan Vineyard and Winery of Sonoma County, California; **73 ph** Alan Williams; **77 b** © Cephas/Steve Elphick; **78–79 ph** Alan Williams; **81 a l** © Cephas/Mick Rock; **80 a r & b ph** Alan Williams; **82** © Cephas/Mick Rock; **84** © Cephas/Mick Rock; **87** © Cephas/Mick Rock; **89** © Cephas/Mick Rock; **90** © Cephas/Nigel Blythe; **92 ph** Alan Williams/Maison M. Chapoutier, Tain l'Hermitage, France; **95** © Cephas/Mick Rock; **96–97** © Cephas/Mick Rock; **99 a l & b ph** Alan Williams; **99 a r** © Cephas/Mick Rock; **102–103** © Cephas/Mick Rock; **105** © Cephas/Herbert Lehmann; **106–107** © Cephas/Mick Rock; **109 all ph** Alan Williams; **110 ph** Alan Williams; **111 ph** Francesca Yorke; **113 ph** Alan Williams; **115** © Cephas/Mick Rock; **117 a l ph** Alan Williams/Chateau Montelena Winery, Napa Valley, California; **117 a r & b ph** Alan Williams; **120–121 ph** Alan Williams/Jordan Vineyard and Winery of Sonoma County, California; **123** © Cephas/Mick Rock; **125** © Cephas/Kevin Argue; **127 a l & a c ph** Alan Williams; **127 b ph** Alan Williams/Errazuriz Don Maximiano Estate, Aconcagua Valley, Chile; **128 a l ph** Alan Williams; **128 a r ph** Alan Williams/Viña Concha y Toro, Maipo Valley, Chile; **128 b ph** Alan Williams/Errazuriz Don Maximiano Estate, Aconcagua Valley, Chile; **130** © Cephas/Matt Wilson; **132–133 ph** Alan Williams; **135 a both ph** Alan Williams; **135 b** © Cephas/Mick Rock; **136** © Cephas/Andy Christodolo; **139 ph** Alan Williams; **140** © Cephas/Kevin Judd; **143** © Cephas/Kevin Judd; **145 a l ph** Alan Williams; **145 a c** © Cephas/Bruce Jenkins; **145 b** © Cephas/Kevin Judd; **146 & 149** © Cephas/Kevin Judd; **151 a l & b** © courtesy of Wines of South Africa; **151 a r ph** Francesca Yorke; **152** © courtesy of Wines of South Africa; **155** © Cephas/Graeme Robinson; **157 a** © Cephas/Mick Rock; **157 b ph** Alan Williams; **159** © courtesy of Symington Family Estates, Portugal; **161** © courtesy of Weinbau-Domäne Schloss Johannisberg/ph Martin Joppen; **162 ph** Francesca Yorke; **163** © courtesy of Weinbau-Domäne Schloss Johannisberg; **165** © Cephas/Andy Christodolo; **166** © Cephas/Mick Rock; **167** © Cephas/Mick Rock; **168 r** © Cephas/Mick Rock; **169** © Cephas/Char Abu Mansoor; **170** © Cephas/Mick Rock; **171 l** © courtesy of Nyetimber Vineyard, England; **171 r ph** Alan Williams.

Business credits

Vineyards, wineries and winegrowers featured in this book:

Ridge Vineyards
17100 Monte Bello Road
Cupertino, CA 95014
USA
T: +1 408 867 3233
wine@ridgewine.com
www.ridgewine.com

Chateau Montelena Winery
1429 Tubbs Lane
Calistoga, CA 94515
USA
T: +1 707 942 5105
www.montelena.com

Jordan Vineyard and Winery
1474 Alexander Valley Road
Healdsburg, CA 95448-9003
USA
T: +1 800 654 1213
www.jordanwinery.com

M.Chapoutier
18 ave du Dr Paul Durand
26600 Tain l'Hermitage
France
T: +33 4 75 08 28 65
chapoutier@chapoutier.com
www.chapoutier.com

New Zealand Winegrowers
Level 3, 52 Symonds St
Auckland
New Zealand
Postal: PO Box 90 276,
Auckland Mail Centre
T: +64 9 303 3527
www.nzwine.com

Nyetimber Vineyard
Gay Street
West Chiltington
West Sussex RH20 2HH
UK
T: +44 (0)1798 813989
info@nyetimber-vineyard.com
www.nyetimber-vineyard.com

Spiral Cellars (UK) Ltd
T: +44 (0)20 8834 7371
www.spiralcellars.com

Symington Family Estates
Travessa Barão de Forrester
4431-702 Villa Nova de Gaia
Portugal
T: +35 1 22 377 6300
www.symington.com

Vina Concha y Toro S.A.
Pirque Casona, Don Melchor Casona and Puente Alto Cellar
Avenida Nueva Tajamar 481
Torre Norte, Piso 15
Las Condos, Santiago
Chile
T: +56 2 476 5000
enquiries@conchaytoro.cl
www.conchaytoro.com

Vina Errazuriz S.A.
Avienda Nueva Tajamar 481
Oficina 503 Torre Sur
Las Condes, Santiago
Chile
T: +56 2 339 9100
www.errazuriz.cl

Weinbau-Domäne Schloss Johannisberg
www.schloss-johannisberg.com

Wines of South Africa
www.wosa.co.za

Australia:
Rockford Vineyards, Barossa Valley, South Australia

Henschke, Barossa Valley, South Australia

Peter Lehmann, Barossa Valley, South Australia

D'Arenberg, McLaren Vale, South Australia

Leeuwin Estate, Margaret River, Western Australia

Spain:
Bodgeas Muga, Haro

La Rioja Alta, Haro

France:
Château Margaux, Pauillac

Château Canon, St Emilion

Château Belair, St Emilion

Château Latour, Pauillac

California:
Beringer Wine Estates, St Helena, Napa Valley

Schramsberg Vineyards, Napa Valley

Heitz Wine Cellars, St Helena, Napa Valley

De Loach Vineyards, Sonoma Valley

Iron Horse Vineyards, Sonoma Valley

The publisher would like to thank the following for supplying wine for photography.

Laithwaites
Laithwaites is a family-owned business that has grown into the most successful mail-order wine merchant in the world. The current range consists of over 3,500 wines from 500 suppliers in 22 different countries. For more information see the website www.laithwaites.co.uk or call 0870 4448282.

Waitrose Wine Direct
0800 188881
www.waitrosewine.com